BREADWINNERS

In recent years the art of home baking has been revived with much enthusiasm. For the cook, there is nothing quite so satisfying as a risen dough followed by the sweet smell of baking bread. In her book, Lesley Bruck introduces the reader to the essential ingredients and the techniques of bread-making. For the beginner she offers a step-by-step guide to baking your first loaf. If you go wrong, Lesley Bruck will tell you how to put it right next time.

A host of recipes collected from all over the world show how there is more to bread-making than a simple everyday loaf. A chapter on festive breads includes many delicious breads which have been baked for centuries to celebrate religious festivals, like the famous Hot Cross Bun. Lesley Bruck also includes recipes for everyday salt breads, sweet tea breads and shows how old or stale bread can be put to mouthwatering use.

Lesley Hewitt Bruck

BREADWINNERS

MAGNUM BOOKS
Methuen Paperbacks Ltd

A Magnum Book

BREADWINNERS
ISBN 0 417 04170 5

First published in 1979
by Magnum Books

Copyright © 1979 by Lesley Hewitt Bruck

Magnum Books are published by
Methuen Paperbacks Ltd
11 New Fetter Lane, London EC4P 4EE

Made and printed in Great Britain by
Hazell Watson & Viney Ltd
Aylesbury, Bucks

The publishers thank The Hamlyn Publishing Group for permission to quote from *Larousse Gastronomique*; Angus & Robertson Publishers for permission to quote from *The Magic Pudding* by Norman Lindsay; and The Macmillan Co. of Australia Pty Ltd for lines from *Journey Among Men* by Jack Marshall and Russell Drysdale.

for my parents Rene and Lance Hewitt

ACKNOWLEDGEMENTS

Kelly King, whose idea it was to write this book; my husband, Jan, for his constant encouragement; my mother-in-law, Leonore, who first taught me about yeast and continental cuisine; lastly, my children Ben, Agnes and Patrick whose steady appraisal of samples kept me going.

CONTENTS

INTRODUCTION

My aim in writing this book is to tell the story of bread and how to make it, for without doubt, it really is the staff of life and has found a place not only on our table and at the altar, but also in much of Western literature. Through the ages bread has had a colourful and changing role to play in our life, from the times when, dipped in honey or olive oil it sustained the foot soldier or was cursed in anger as being the bread of affliction, idleness, and sometimes deceit, to the present day when it keeps the scientist awake at night wondering over the opposing values of different grains. It is the food we reach for when hungry – and most likely therefore, to be the first item struck from the dieter's menu. Even the word itself has come to mean 'money' in modern English usage.

The exact origin of bread is unknown, but most historians agree that it was an Egyptian invention arising out of carelessness. Mrs Beeton, in her monumental work *Beeton's Book of Household Management*, which was destined to revolutionize Victorian housekeeping, remarked:

'... about the beginning of the thirtieth Olympiad, the slave of an archon, at Athens, made leavened bread by accident. He had left some wheaten dough in an earthen pan, and forgotten it; some days afterwards, he lighted upon it again, and found it turning sour. His first thought was to throw it away; but, his master coming up, he mixed this now acescant dough with some fresh dough which he was working at. The bread thus produced was found delicious by the archon and his friends; and the slave, being summoned and catechised, told the secret. It spread all over Athens; and everybody wanting levened bread at once, certain persons set up as bread-makers, or bakers. In a short time bread-making became quite an art, and, "Athenian bread" was quoted all over Greece as the best bread, just as the honey of Hymettus was celebrated as the best honey.'

The availability of cereal crops has always affected the production of bread, and so the quality and price of a loaf have always reflected the prevailing state of an economy, the volume of the harvest, and a society's cultural tradition and tastes. In Europe, a poor harvest or the advent of war were bound to affect bread prices and consequently history has often seen the introduction of strict controls over the price of grain, with harsh penalties for those who infringed such laws. In such a way, economists then as now try to strike a balance between supply, demand and need, thereby keeping the threat of famine under check. In our affluent Western society it is very easy to lose sight of starvation as a reality, but it is always just around the corner, as charity drives such as 'Bread for the World' and our occasional glimpses into the life styles of the developing countries remind us.

Over the centuries the art of bread-making has seen little change, but with the introduction of leaven to the bread loaf, we have added to its variety by the addition of new flour strains and, as the standard of living began to rise right across Europe, the inclusion of spices, fruit and nuts. Sorghum, and later wheat and rye, were the common bread grains and, up till quite recently the usage of wheat or rye flour differentiated the rich from the poor. The paler, innermost part of the wheat grain can only be obtained by successive bolting or sieving, making it less plentiful and in times gone by this earmarked it for the wealthy, leaving the darker, coarser flour for the worker and peasant. Habit dies hard, and it is interesting to note that in Central Europe, white bread is frequently reserved for the holy day, Sunday.

The Jewish and Christian religions have played a large part in diversifying our bread, from the time when manna fell from heaven on earth through to the present day when consecrated wafers are accepted as part of the communion rite. As the staple item of diet, bread was adorned for special feast days so that the symbolic meaning of religion was expressed in our food, as when the sign of the cross is made on Easter Hot Cross buns. Other important occasions in life such as birth, marriage, death, or victory at war, came to be commemorated with the baking of special and elaborate loafs, for example, the Crailsheimer Horaffen of Germany.

In recent years there has been a renewed interest in our diet, partly as a result of Western obesity having become as serious a problem as the starvation of the Third World. The spotlight has thus been turned on to improving grain production around the globe, as cereal crops can provide us with a sound and economic alternative to meat in providing our protein requirements. There is also a growing awareness of the value of wholemeal flours – those in which the husk as well as the kernel of the grain are retained in milling – and as well, we are learning to think in terms of variety when we select flour for bread-baking.

Chapter One

SEPARATING THE WHEAT
FROM THE CHAFF

INSTRUCTIONS ON BREAD-MAKING

THE BASIC INGREDIENTS FOR THE MAKING of bread are flour, water, salt and yeast, mixed normally in the ratio of:450g (1lb) flour: 15g (½oz) yeast: ¼ litre (½ pint) water: ¾ table-spoon salt. This ratio can vary according to climate, the type of grain milled to make the flour and the time of year. For this reason, the making of a good loaf of bread will depend largely on adapting the given quantities in any given recipe to suit the conditions prevailing where you live. We will now take a look at the components used in bread-making and discuss the techniques of proving, kneading and baking.

FLOUR is finely ground grain and can be obtained from many different cereals, wheat being the most versatile and possessing the highest gluten content, which provides a loaf with a stable 'framework' and elasticity. For this reason, a little wheaten flour is included in almost all breads. Next in popularity is rye, which renders a darker, more aromatic flour, much prized in Central Europe. Cornmeal or polenta is the yellow flour of the maize plant and a native of Northern America introduced to the Western world after colonization of the New World. Buckwheat is a black, triangular grain which came to Europe from Russia and later became popular in America. Other flours sometimes used in bread-making include oaten flour, millet, barley, potato, rice, soyabean, lentil and pea. Perhaps the strangest flour of all is found in the Australian Outback – that of the nardoo plant. The

Burke and Wills expedition of the nineteenth century which
crossed the continent from south to north was kept alive by
reaping this grain and pounding it to a flour which they
subsequently made into flat cakes in the manner of the
aborigines.

To obtain the flour the grain must first be ground and then
winnowed to separate the outer husk from the inner kernel.
There are several grades of fineness in ground grain, from
the coarsest 'crack' and 'grits', through 'meals', to the finest
'flour'. Flour which is designated as being 'wholemeal' includes the whole grain and not just the ground inner kernel.
As the outer parts or 'bran' contain more gluten, a wholemeal flour is a much 'stronger' flour and produces a loaf with
more body. In days gone by, Russian flour was held as being
the finest and best and was consequently much sought after
by the famous bakeries. Today the Canadian strain known as
'Manatoba' commands the highest price amongst the wheat-
en flours on the world market. Because of their rarity, rye,
oaten, and other flours tend to be expensive, so the best plan
for the home baker is to buy flour in bulk from a mill. If you
plan to purchase flour in large amounts, make sure before-
hand that you have the means to store it, as it will rapidly
become a home for weevils and moths unless it is stored in
an air-tight container, which protects it from dampness at
the same time. The Greeks stored flour in clay pits underground, but a simple plastic bag or plastic dustbin with a
clip-on lid will suffice. If you discover strange silken threads
in your flour it means that some insect or other has already
moved in – in which case, sift through the flour and re-seal
tightly.

MILK AND WATER provide the moisture necessary for
yeast growth. They are always warmed before being brought
in contact with the yeast: in the case of fresh yeast, at a
temperature of 40–45°C/104–113°F; and in the case of dried
and processed yeast, somewhat higher. If you are using un-
pasteurised milk, scald it before cooling and adding the yeast,

as this will destroy certain bacteria which attack the yeast flora. Sometimes powdered milk, sour cream, or buttermilk are used as alternatives to milk and water.

SALT. The salt of the earth is a precious commodity, so prized by our forefathers that they sometimes commissioned such goldsmiths as Cellini to craft elaborate and magnificent cellars to house it. The Romans fell upon English salt with glee during their imperial reign over that country and brought it back to Rome by the shipload. Whether you pronounce the word 'solt' or 'sault' it will still have the same effect on your dough, which is to regulate yeast growth and bring out the flavour of the grain.

FATS such as margarine, butter, lard, oil, and bacon or even goose fat are added to the dough as a means of making the crumb tender and resilient, and at the same time improving its keeping qualities. If faced with a choice between butter and margarine, I always opt for butter – you know where you stand and it tastes better in the long run – but it is equally possible to use any of the margarines on the market.

EGGS bind the dough and lend it a cake-like flavour. They first made their appearance in yeast breads when the standard of living rose, enabling the peasantry to add a touch of richness to their festive loaves. They also help bind the dough and give it elasticity. If a bland, tasteless glaze is needed on a loaf, a mixture of beaten eggs and milk, or plain egg yolk is ideal.

SUGAR and its counterparts molasses and honey, which were commonly used when sugar was too expensive, provide the growing yeast plant with its food, and for this reason often a little sugar is included in salt loaves.

SPICES. With the discovery of an Eastern sea route in the early part of the sixteenth century, an alternative and cheaper route to the great spice reserves of the East was opened up.

Prior to this, spices had been trickled into Europe by the un-reliable path of the camel track which wound its way west-wards from the Middle East to the gateway of Venice. For a long time the spice trade – such as it was – remained under the sole control of the large German finance house of Fugger, with the result that spice prices were kept very high, and Europe's purse strings were drawn tight against the outside market. It was common for putrid meat to be disguised under a mantle of pepper: the sweet spices were usually re-served for the more glorious purpose of embellishing festive cakes and loaves, and for burning as incense on holy days.

FRUITS AND NUTS are found in sweet tea loaves and the richer type of symbolic breads to be found in Chapter 5. They are frequently ground or chopped to release their flavour into the dough.

LEAVENING AGENTS. Some breads are unleavened, but most doughs have some form of leaven in them for the simple reason that a lighter bread is more easily digested and aesthetically more pleasing to the eye. In the Bible leaven has connotations of evil, as its nature is to permeate every-thing with which it comes in contact. This is the meaning behind the words 'a little leaven leavens the whole lump', and in point of fact this is true in a literal sense as well, be-cause too much yeast has a souring effect on the dough. The discovery of yeast has been described by Mrs Beeton already in the introduction to this book. The type of fermentation which such ancient races employed was panary fermenta-tion, brought about in much the same way in which we pre-pare sour-dough today, sometimes with the addition of wine dregs. The usual leavening agent is yeast, which is a living plant present in the air we breathe. It is a delicate plant which perishes easily if not kept under optimum conditions –

'Yeast can be quite a beast,
that daren't be tickled or teased,

> but if greased and then warmed
> it is bound soon to swarm,
> and prove to be king of the feast.'

THE AUTHOR

Bearing this good advice in mind, keep yeast at an even temperature during proving and do not let the temperature rise beyond 50°C/122°F, as it will die. When buying yeast, prove its freshness by smelling it: it should be beery and sweet, with a creamy colour and moist skin. Dried yeast is available in packets and is less susceptible to heat than fresh yeast, but its age can never be verified and it is possible to buy a supply which is totally defunct. Dried yeast has half the weight of fresh yeast, so if you use dried yeast for any of the recipes in this book, halve the amount given for fresh yeast.

If you want to make your own 'wild yeast', here is a recipe:

1 *small handful of hops*	3 *tablespoons flour*
1 *litre (1¾ pint) water*	3 *tablespoons sugar*

Boil the hops in the water for 20 minutes or until the hops sink to the bottom of the saucepan. Strain and allow to cool. Blend the flour and sugar, using a little of the hop mixture. Add the rest of the hop liquor and stir well. Bottle and seal securely and stand in a warm place. After 24–36 hours the yeast will be ready to use.

Sour-dough starter is also a means of aerating or leavening bread dough. A little moistened flour is allowed to sour after which it can be kneaded into unleavened dough to aerate it, or used in conjunction with yeast. Early Alaskan settlers and trappers kept special strains of sour-dough at a constant temperature by tucking it between their bare skin and clothes, thus ensuring that the soured dough would not die from the cold. The preparation of sour-dough is given under SCHWÄBISCHES BAUERNBROT (p. 96).

Baking powder and soda, and cream of tartar are used for quick breads when the lengthy process of proving needs to be side-stepped. These breads are drier than yeast breads and an aftertaste of salts cannot be avoided.

Stiffly beaten egg white is sometimes added to small white bread rolls to make the dough very light, in which case less liquid is used in the dough.

Before you start to make your own bread, collect a few necessary utensils, namely a large wooden board or table; a bread knife with a long, narrow serrated blade; a set of mixing bowls; a measuring cup which has gradations for weights-by-volume for flour, sugar and dried fruit; a skewer; a thermometer to train your appreciation of temperature variation; a cooling rack (disused oven racks are useful); and, last but not least, a few baking tins – round, loaf, ring, tubular, biscuit tray, and a few terracotta pot plants. Keep the tins clean, and when not in use wipe out with a little sweet almond oil to prevent rusting.

Techniques of Bread-Making

1. *Mixing and Proving*

Ideally, all ingredients to be incorporated into the bread should be of the same temperature, even the bowl in which they are to be mixed. In winter or in a cold country this is particularly important, as the slightest draught or drop in temperature can jeopardize yeast growth or even kill it altogether. The flour can be warmed by placing it in the bowl in the oven after sifting. When it feels comfortably warm to the hand, it is ready to use. It is not necessary to do this in a warm climate. It is a wise precaution to buy a thermometer and learn the feel of 35°C/95°F, the temperature at which the yeast starts to multiply. If you plunge your hand into water of this temperature it will feel slightly warm. Proving is the period during which yeast grows. During its growth the plant cells feed on sugar and give off alcohol (the principle of fermentation, and the reason why the dough smells like wine), and carbon dioxide as waste products. This gas collects in bubbles in the dough, causing it to rise. During baking both the alcohol and carbon dioxide are burnt off, leaving cavities in the space they occupied. The process of yeast growth is triggered off by the introduction of moisture and food to the yeast cells – the warmth only serves to accelerate the process, it is not essential, but once it has been applied it cannot be withdrawn. If you want dough to prove very slowly, place in the refrigerator, and this will keep the rate of growth of the yeast at a sluggish minimum. It is even possible to prove the dough in an icy pail of water – when it is ready it floats to the surface. Assuming that you have chosen to speed the proving up as much as possible, you will now need to find a warm place to rest the dough. Our cat greatly helped me to find an ideal spot one fine summer day when she walked straight to a ceramic roofing tile which was propped against the wall of the house in a sunny corner. I laid the tile flat and found that the sun's heat concentrated in it to just the right degree. Unless your oven has a very fine thermostat adjustment, I would not recommend proving dough in it till you become quite skilled at bread-making as it is very easy to burn and kill the yeast this way. A drying cupboard is a good spot, or the plate warmer under a stove. In winter dough can be covered and steamed in a bowl over hot water to make it rise. In summer it will be sufficient just to cover the dough and leave at room temperature. Whatever you decide on, remember that the quickest rise will take upwards of half an hour in optimum conditions. When the dough is adequately proved, two fingers pressed into it will leave two impressions which do not rise up when the fingers are withdrawn.

With practice you will learn to be patient, and become swift without being deadly.

2. *Kneading*

Kneading is the action of combining all the bread ingredients to make a smooth dough, and is repeated once, twice, or three times during the preparation of the dough. In commercial bakeries kneading is performed by large machines, and at home you can knead with the help of a domestic mixer if it is fitted with a dough hook. It is pleasant work however to do by hand and you will soon learn the rhythm – rather like scything grass.

Before you start to knead the dough, combine the ingredients in the bowl with your hand, a wooden spoon or whisk. Then lift the dough out on to a floured board and proceed to knead by lifting the dough which is furthest from you and folding it forward on itself and push away. To knead for a lengthy period – and most recipes require 8–10 minutes – it may be easier for you to stand on the telephone directory or a low stool so that you can lean on to the dough with stiffened elbows without tiring yourself. Gradually you will feel the dough changing texture and becoming smoother – even silky to the touch – and elastic. At this stage the kneading is beginning to have its effect, which is to release the gluten locked in the flour particles by continual bruising. Some doughs are too wet to knead, e.g. in the case of some yeast-batter breads, but the same end is achieved by slapping or beating the dough. If you are called away during kneading cover the dough ball with an up-turned basin to prevent draughts from chilling it. Sometimes it is necessary to knead large quantities of dough at a time, when, for example you are baking ten or more loaves to last for a few weeks (in Scandinavia bread is baked in large quantities in autumn to last over winter and is strung up in the rafters over the kitchen). This is well nigh impossible unless you are possessed of Gargantuan strength, but here is one remedy: inscriptions and engravings on the tomb of Rameses II show slaves kneading dough with their feet. I can see no objection to this! Clean the bath, and sprinkle with flour. Load the dough into the tub and proceed to knead with the feet.

Once the dough is smooth roll it into a ball and grease lightly or simply cover with a cloth which prevents a crust from developing during proving. When the dough has doubled in bulk it is ready for the second kneading which distributes the carbon dioxide gas released during proving. Before kneading a second time 'punch down' or 'knock' the dough by punching into its centre. This expels excess gas from the dough, enabling it to form a finer texture during the second proving. Now knead the dough lightly for a few minutes before proving a second time.

3. *Shaping*

Dough can be formed by baking it in a mould or baking 'free', i.e. without the aid of a tin or mould. At first it is not easy to form and control the final shape that the loaf will take, so keep the free type of loaf small until you are more skilled. All loaves to be baked free require a little extra flour to stiffen the dough and prevent spreading. Experiment with decorative plaits of two, three, four and six strands before trying them out on the dough. If plaiting a long strand, start from the centre and plait to the end, then turn the strand and plait underhand in the opposite direction – this prevents the braid from distorting. Plait loosely to allow for expansion during proving.

If baking two loaves in one tin, shape them separately, and to make for easy separation after baking, brush a little melted fat over the edges where the dough touches.

4. *Glazing*

An egg glaze is applied after the dough has risen, to allow the dough to 'breathe' during proving.

Sugar glazes are usually applied after the loaf leaves the oven.

Gelatine glaze (1 teaspoon gelatine dissolved with 2 teaspoons sugar and brought to the boil in 1 cup water) is applied while the loaf is still warm.

Cornflour glaze (1 teaspoon cornflour thickened by warming in ½ cup water) is applied 5 minutes before the bread is due to leave the oven.

5. *Baking*

Conversion tables for baking temperatures are given at the end of the book. As a general rule, small loaves and rolls are baked at 220 to 230°C/425 to 450°F and larger loaves at a somewhat lower temperature 200°C/400°F. Always preheat the oven to 230°C/450°F and lower the temperature when the bread is put in the oven, as the temperature drops when the oven door is opened. Grease all pans before filling with dough, and if the bread browns prematurely, cover with foil to prevent scorching. To create even warmth in your oven you can lay terracotta tiles over the oven racks to form a tile floor. If baking only one loaf, place it in the middle of the oven to promote an even rise. The following table lists the changes in the dough as its temperature rises:

35°C/95°F . . .	yeast starts to multiply
40–45°C/104–113°F . .	peak of yeast growth
52°C/126°F . . .	yeast dies
65°C/149°F . . .	enzyme activity ceases
75°C/167°F . . .	alcohol evaporates
100°C/212°F . . .	steam rises
120°C/248°F . . .	golden crust
180°C/356°F . . .	russet crust
200°C/392°F . . .	charcoal formation

Test for a finished loaf by tapping its base: if it has baked long enough it will sound hollow.

6. *Cooling*

Cool all loaves on racks once they leave the oven. This prevents trapped steam making the base of the bread soggy.

7. *Freezing*

All types of bread can be frozen. Select airtight containers such as plastic tubs or bags so that the flavour will not be affected by other foods in the freezer. Expel as much air as possible from the container before sealing. Sliced bread can be wrapped a few slices at a time, which makes separation of the slices easy. Uncooked dough can be frozen, but leave it time to thaw and prove before baking. If frozen cooked bread is needed in a hurry, place in a hot oven for 20 minutes.

8. *Freshening a Stale Loaf*
Hold briefly under a running tap and bake briefly in a hot oven; be careful not to burn.

And so to the recipes. My suggestion is to begin with the first two, *Basic White Bread* and *Pain de Mie*. At the end of the recipe for Pain de Mie there is a list of possible errors you may have made in baking your first loaf, and the remedy.

BASIC WHITE BREAD
Loaf and Harvest Sheaf

This is a basic bread recipe in which only wheaten flour is used. It has been placed at the beginning of the book because each step is clearly explained. I suggest you make it the first time as a loaf, using a bread pan, and the second time as a free form loaf, the Harvest Sheaf, because it is only through practice and repetition that you will learn to discern a soft dough from a firm one, and a dough which is too sticky from one which is too dry. At the end of the next recipe – Pain de Mie – there is a list of possible faults which you may be able to find in the finished bread. Study them and read the first chapter again and try once more. After a little practice you will be confident and successful.

500g (1lb 2oz) strong plain flour	10–12g (⅓–½oz) fresh yeast
1 teaspoon salt	¼ litre (½ pint) lukewarm water

Sift the flour and salt into a large bowl. If the weather is cold let the bowl stand at room temperature for a while. Press a well into the centre of the flour. Dissolve the yeast in a little warm water and pour into the well. Stir, drawing in a little flour from the edges, and then combine thoroughly with the flour. Using the hand or a wooden spoon, gradually add the water. If you propose to bake the dough in a loaf tin, the dough should be soft but not sticky. If the dough is to be shaped into a harvest sheaf add a little more flour at this stage to make a stiffer dough. Turn out on to a floured board or table and begin to knead the dough as given under 'Kneading' (p. 20). If it is very sticky, before adding more flour see if you can do the first few turns of the dough by lifting it with a spatula. If the dough does not become more workable add extra flour, a tablespoon at a time, during the kneading till it has taken up as much as it needs not to stick to your fingers. If the dough is rigid and very stiff, add a little extra liquid, which will adjust its texture. Once the dough is smooth and elastic, roll into a ball and grease lightly on all sides. Return to the clean bowl and set in a warm place free of draughts. Let the dough prove till it is doubled in bulk, or till two fingers pressed into the dough leave two hollows which do not spring back when the fingers are withdrawn. Punch down the dough with the closed fist to collapse it, and knead again for about one minute. Shape as desired, or fill bread pans to two-thirds their height with the dough. Cover and prove again till double in bulk. Bake in a hot oven – 200°C/400°F – till golden and the base of the loaves emit a hollow sound when tapped.

How to form a Harvest Sheaf:
1. Divide the dough into 9 equal parts.
2. Shape 8 of these parts into ropes and slash twice along half the length of the rope.
3. Plait the slashed ends and then arrange the ropes together, laying the plaits side-by-side. Fan out the plaited parts of the end ropes to form the 'ears'.

4. Shape the ninth part into a twisted rope and bind round the centre of the sheaf.

PAIN DE MIE
French Sandwich Loaf

Pain de Mie is the basic Square French sandwich loaf which is ideal for making sandwiches, toast, canapés, croûtons and little hors d'oeuvres. It is baked in a special sandwich loaf tin which is fitted with a sliding roof, but if you do not have one of these, simply cover the risen dough with greased foil and close off the top of the tin with weighted tiles or a baking sheet.

900g (2lb) flour	*2 teaspoons sugar*
1 tablespoon coarse salt	*100g (4oz) unsalted butter*
30g (1oz) fresh yeast	*⅜ litre (¼pint) warm water*

Sift all but a little of the flour into a large bowl. Scatter the salt over the surface of the flour. Dissolve the yeast and 2 teaspoons sugar in a little of the warm water, cover and allow to stand until the yeast starts to bubble. Take the butter in both hands and, holding it over the flour in the bowl, squeeze it between the fingers till pieces drop off into the flour. Add half the water to the yeast mixture, stirring well. Pour the yeast into the centre of the flour and work in enough of the remaining water to make a stiff, sticky dough. Turn out on to a floured board and place the remaining flour on the edge of the board. Knead the dough very vigorously, adding more flour if necessary. Continue to knead and bang the dough for 10 minutes – by this stage it will be elastic and very smooth. Roll into a ball, grease lightly and place in a covered bowl to prove till double in bulk. Punch down the dough and let rest in the bowl for 5 minutes. Remove from the bowl and knead briefly a second time. Return to the bowl and prove again till double in bulk. Punch down and knead briefly a third time. Punch down the dough and fit into a closed loaf pan so that the dough half fills the greased pan. Cover with a cloth and let rise till almost doubled in bulk. Grease the inside of the lid (or foil) and slide home over the loaf. Bake at 190°C/375°F for about 50 minutes, rotating the tin during baking so that all sides of the pain de mie are evenly browned. Remove the loaf from the pan and test the loaf by tapping on its base. Return to the warm oven briefly so that the crust will acquire an all-over golden colour. Cool before slicing.

What Went Wrong?

'He invented water-mills, windmills, hand-mills, and a myriad other contrivances, to grind his grain and reduce it to flour, invented leaven to ferment the dough and salt to give it flavour – for he knew very well that nothing in the world renders human beings more subject to ailments than the employment of unfermented, unsalted bread. He also invented fire to bake with and clocks and dials to mark the time that his bread, which is the creature of grain, took in baking.'

RABELAIS OF PANTAGRUEL

Pantagruel loved his bread and in the passage above, warns the baker that bread made without salt or leaven can lead to untold human ailments. Other things can go wrong with bread as well, so take an honest look at a slice of your first loaf, analyse its texture and appearance, and learn to remedy it!

1. If the slice is soggy and heavy, this can be due to fermentation having gone on for too long, which makes the dough collapse in on itself. If the slice is damp but not heavy, baking time was too short – next time leave the bread in the oven till it sounds hollow when tapped on the base.

2. If a space develops between the upper crust and the body

of the loaf it is usually due to rapid rising of the upper layers once in the oven because the loaf was not formed tightly enough, e.g. in the case of rolled French breads. If there is a similar hollow at the base, the oven was too hot initially. Take heart, this is not serious: there is an old German saying that says that the baker's soul is housed in the hollow.

3. If the loaf baked was a free form loaf and the slice looks very wide and short-legged, the dough was too soft to be able to 'climb up itself'. Add a little extra flour to the loaf to be baked free and this will not happen a second time..

4. The most common error is the heavy, dense slice – a direct result of impatience: let the dough prove longer next time till two fingers inserted in the risen dough leave two impressions which do not spring up. If you are using a recipe where a definite proving time is given, remember that it refers to optimal conditions only, which almost never exist.

5. Larousse tells us that
   'the holes in it [the crumb, or soft part of the slice] should be uneven, not too big – which is a sign of badly-kneaded dough – nor too small – which is a sign of insufficient fermentation; the smell should be sweet, the taste clean and pleasant.'
However, if your slice is from a loaf of French bread, the large holes are typical of this bread.

6. If the crust is pale and starts to tear when you are cutting the examination slice, return the bread to the oven and rotate it so that all sides come in contact with direct heat.

7. If the loaf is lop-sided but your oven is level, and the slice has a crumb of uneven texture, then the dough was probably placed to one side of the oven, thereby causing an uneven air flow. If baking only one loaf be sure to place it in the middle of the oven unless otherwise stated.

8. If the bread has cracked open on the side or top, it will be a strange but certainly very good loaf – bravo!

9. If your loaf came out of the oven with a golden domed

crust, and on slicing proved to have an even soft crumb and crisp crusts, the loaf is a perfect success and you are spared the medieval punishment meted out to the bakers of inferior bread, which was to be publicly whipped or pilloried.

Chapter Two

'PANEM ET CIRCENSES' – BREAD AND CIRCUSES

RECIPES FOR FESTIVE AND SYMBOLIC BREADS

As NECESSITY IS THE MOTHER OF invention, so too is boredom the precursor of fantasy. No doubt ancient cooks found themselves in this dilemma when faced by ravenous or jaded appetites. They rose nobly to the occasion, presenting their guests with successive culinary mutations – even in the matter of bread.

So now let us invite the festive loaf to our table, and while we enjoy it let it also remind us of a world we are losing.

Lent and Easter Breads

KRAPFEN
Doughnuts with Rosehip Jam

Krapfen originated as a symbolic bread for the Fastnacht, Fasching or Mardigras, the period of feasting before the long lean days of Lent which lead up to Easter. Throughout Europe this 'Carnival' is celebrated for up to four weeks, with masked balls, and light-hearted gaiety which makes the Anglo-Saxon 'Pancake', or 'Shrove' Tuesday pale by comparison. Even children take part in the festivities, and can be seen in fancy-dress costume gathered around immense baker's trays of Krapfen clamouring to secure their share of the warm and sugary treats.

600g (1lb 5oz) flour
30g (1oz) fresh yeast
¼ litre (½ pint) milk
100g (4oz) sugar
85g (3oz) butter

2 eggs
pinch salt
grated rind one half lemon
rosehip jam

Sift the flour into a bowl and press a well into the middle.
Crumble the yeast, and place it in the well together with a
little of the milk heated to lukewarm and one teaspoon sugar.
Stir the yeast and milk to form a paste, drawing in a little of
the flour from the sides. Cover and prove for 20 minutes.
Soften the butter in the rest of the milk and add it together
with the other ingredients, except the jam, to the flour in the
bowl. Beat the mixture vigorously with a spoon till the dough
leaves the sides of the bowl, then turn out on to a lightly
floured board and knead for 5 minutes. Cover the dough
and prove till double in bulk. Punch down and roll out to a
thickness of about 1cm (½in). Using a scone-cutter with a
diameter of 7½cm (3in), stamp out as many rounds as possible. Place a little rosehip jam in the centre of half the rounds
and cover each with another round. Press the edges firmly
together to make a sphere. Pile the Krapfen on a tray, cover
them and prove till light and puffy.

Heat vegetable oil in a deep saucepan or deep-fryer to
180°C/356°F and deep fry the Krapfen a few at a time till
they are golden on both sides. While still hot roll in icing
sugar or ice with vanilla icing. Serve warm.

LOKMADES (Cyprus)

These deep-fried yeast balls are known variously as *Loukoum-
ades* in Crete and as *Lokmades* in Cyprus. They are eaten
prior to Lent at Carnival time and served warm, dipped in
either honey or cinnamon. Their origin is most likely an
ancient one, as the Greeks were the first race to develop a
'cuisine' as we understand it today. They gave birth to many

famous chefs whose art was much prized by the new Roman
civilization. Story has it that the chef's hat, being conical, is
derived from the Greek priest's mitre.

675g (1½lb) flour   2 teaspoons salt
20g (⅔oz) fresh yeast   2 tablespoons oil
warm water

Sift the flour into a large bowl and press a well into the
centre. Crumble the yeast into the well and add enough
warm water to make a paste. Stir the yeast and water, drawing in enough flour from the sides of the well to make a paste.
Cover, and allow the yeast to 'sponge' for 20 minutes.
Sprinkle the salt over the flour and stir in enough warm
water to make a soft but not sticky dough. Add the oil, and
work the dough with the hand till it is incorporated. Turn
out on to a floured board and knead till smooth and elastic.
Cover and prove. Using two wet teaspoons, form the dough
into small balls and deep fry several at a time. Drain on
absorbent paper and serve warm, together with a bowl of
ground cinnamon and one of honey to dip the lokmades in
before eating.

HAMAN'S EARS (Jewish)

These pastries are eaten as part of the Jewish festival of
Purim which falls shortly before Nisan or the Passover on
March 14. They commemorate the deliverance of the Jewish
people from the hands of the betrayer Haman by Mordecai
and Esther, who later became Queen. They are shaped in
the form of an ear and leavened by the inclusion of baking
powder in the ingredients.

250g (9oz) flour   warm water
1 teaspoon baking powder   oil for deep frying
pinch salt   icing sugar
2 eggs

Sift the flour and baking powder into a bowl. Add the salt and eggs and enough warm water to make a cohesive dough. Roll out the dough to a thickness of about $\frac{1}{2}$cm ($\frac{1}{4}$in), and cut into strips measuring 2cm × 12cm (1in × 4$\frac{1}{2}$in). Fry the strips in oil heated to 90°C/104°F till they are puffed and golden. Twist immediately into ear shapes and place on absorbent paper to drain. Dust the ears with powdered icing sugar.

MATZOS (Jewish)

'. . . ye shall eat unleavened bread. Seven days shall there be no leaven found in your houses.'

The Bible, Exodus Ch. 12, *v.* 18–19

'And the people took the dough before it was leavened, their kneading troughs being bound up in their clothes upon their shoulders.'

Exodus Ch. 12, *v.* 34

Long before the birth of Christ and Christianity an angel of God passed over Egypt at midnight, killing all the firstborn of the land bar those of Jewish descent. The Pharaoh was frightened and gladly consented to allow the Jews to leave Egypt. Under the leadership of Moses some 600,000 men, women and children started their long journey in search of Canaan, the Promised Land, the land of milk and honey. The Pharaoh suffered a change of heart and gave chase to the Jews, but he and his soldiers perished in the sea and the Israelites continued their flight. Today, the feast of the Passover or Pesach commemorates this flight with the eating of unleavened bread or 'Matzos'. It is of prime importance in the Jewish religion, and during this period only certain foods may be eaten and special utensils are reserved for their preparation.

250g (9oz) matzo meal *enough water to make a soft*
salt *paste*

Knead the meal and salt with enough water to make a soft paste. Roll out thinly into rounds or squares and prick all over. Transfer the bread to baking sheets and bake at 180°C/350°F till crisp.

VETEKRANS (Sweden)

Vetekrans is the king of the Swedish Easter loaves. It is spiced with cardamom and cinnamon, rolled in layers and slashed to reveal a filling of almonds, spiced brown sugar and fruit.

750g (1lb 11oz) flour
½ teaspoon salt
½ teaspoon cardamom
½ teaspoon cinnamon
300ml (½ pint) milk and
  water
85g (3oz) butter
50g (2oz) fresh yeast
100g (4oz) sugar
1 egg white

Filling
125g (4½oz) mixed fruits
50g (2oz) brown sugar
2 tablespoons flaked almonds

Glaze
1 beaten egg
coarse sugar
2 tablespoons sliced almonds

Sift the flour, salt, cardamom and cinnamon into a large bowl. Press a well into the centre of the flour. Scald the milk and water, remove from the heat and dissolve the butter in it. Allow to cool to lukewarm and pour into the well in the flour. Cream the yeast and sugar together and stir into the liquid, drawing in a little flour from the sides of the well. Cover the bowl and set aside for a few minutes in a warm place. Beat all the ingredients together, adjusting the amount of liquid or flour in the dough to make a soft but not sticky dough. Turn out on to a floured board and knead for 5 minutes. Roll the dough into a ball and place in a greased bowl. Turn the dough to coat with grease on all sides. Cover and prove till double in bulk. Meanwhile, prepare the filling:

mix the ingredients thoroughly and set aside. When the dough is risen, punch down and knead lightly. Divide into three pieces of equal size. Roll each piece into a long strip 20cm × 60cm (8in × 24in). Spread a third of the filling on each strip and place the strips on top of each other. Roll up into a sausage from the long side, sealing the flap with a little egg white. Bend the sausage into a wreath and join as carefully as possible, sealing the overriding end with egg white. Transfer to a greased baking sheet. Using scissors, slash the wreath evenly from the outside, cutting almost through to the centre, about twenty times. Turn each slice so that the filling shows. Cover with a cloth and prove till doubled in bulk. Bake at 200°C/400°F for 45 minutes or until almost golden. 10 minutes before baking is finished, brush quickly with beaten egg and sprinkle with sugar and almonds. Return to oven till shiny and the almonds are delicately browned.

The Russian Orthodox celebration of Easter is one which is of great importance in the year, and culminates in the midnight mass after which families return to their homes for the joyous Easter feast. The stately cylindrical bread, Kulich, and a creamy rich pyramid-shaped cheese, Pashka, are intrinsic to the celebration. Shawled matriachs carry the Kulich, wrapped in linen, to the cathedral where it is blessed. The towering breads are unwrapped and adorned with a single red taper which is then lit.

For the well-to-do Russian, the Easter feast begins with vodka and such appetite-whetters as caviar, liver pâté and fish in aspic. Next comes ham baked in rye dough or perhaps spicy sausage, cold duck and pickles, zakuska kolbase, hors d'oeuvres and roast goose or pork. In a place of honour, for the conclusion of the feast, is the Kulich, dotted with liqueur raisins. It is joined by the candied fruit and almond filled Pashka (which is also the Russian word for Easter).

PASHKA (Russia)

100g (4oz) sweet butter
½ cup castor sugar
3 egg yolks
500g (1lb 2oz) ricotta,
   cottage cheese or Quark
1 teaspoon vanilla

grated rind of one lemon
½ cup chopped glacé fruits
½ cup finely chopped almonds
¼ cup currants
¼ cup chopped mixed peel
½ cup whipped cream

Cream the butter with the castor sugar till fluffy. Add the
egg yolks one at a time, beating well after each addition.
Force the cheese through a sieve or put in the blender till
smooth, then beat with the butter mixture. Add the vanilla
and lemon rind. Mix in the fruits, almonds and mixed peel.
Fold in the whipped cream and shape the pashka into a
pyramid with the aid of a spatula. In Russia the letters
'X B', which in the Cyrillic alphabet stand for 'Christos
voskre' or 'Christ is risen', are marked on the sides. The
letters can be defined with angelica or tiny strips of glacé
fruits. Chill the pashka before serving.

KULICH (Russia)

⅛ litre (¼ pint) milk
30g (1oz) fresh yeast
200g (7oz) butter
60g (2oz) sugar
1 tablespoon grated lemon
   rind
1 teaspoon salt
2 eggs

4 egg yolks
650g (1lb 7oz) flour
½ cup raisins
½ cup sultanas
¼ cup rum
½ cup blanched, toasted,
   chopped almonds
vanilla icing

Scald the milk and allow to cool to lukewarm. Dissolve the
yeast in the milk together with one teaspoon sugar. In a
large bowl combine the butter, sugar, lemon rind, and salt.

Add the yeast mixture to this and the eggs and egg yolks. Gradually beat in enough of the flour to make a soft but not sticky dough. Gather the dough into a ball and turn it out on to a lightly floured working surface. Work in the remaining flour and knead till the dough is satiny. Form into a ball, coat with butter by turning in a buttered bowl, cover and allow to prove till double in bulk. While the dough is rising, plump the raisins and sultanas in the rum by heating them together in a saucepan. Drain the fruit and dry it, then dust with a little flour. Punch down the dough and knead it lightly. Incorporate the fruit and almonds into the dough as you knead. Grease a large cylindrical tin and tie a greased collar on to the rim, in the manner of making a soufflé, to allow for rising. Place the dough into the tin, and allow to prove till double in bulk. Bake at 180–190°C/350–375°F for 50–60 minutes. Cool the kulich on a rack, and then ice the top with vanilla icing. Decorate the top with red paper roses, and serve with pashka.

In Greece, both on the mainland and the surrounding islands, Easter coincides with the coming of Spring. At this time the almond trees are covered in white blossom and the air is heady with their perfume and that of lemon and pine trees. Holy Saturday, the Saturday preceding Easter Sunday, is a very busy one for the housewives preparing for the feast which is held after the midnight mass marking the end of Lent. In the early evening families congregate for the procession to church, each carrying a lighted candle which is carefully shielded from the wind. Towards the end of the service, shortly before midnight, all the candles in the church are dimmed and the priest intones the words 'Christos Anesti', meaning 'Christ is risen', after which the people return home to their feasting. The meal is a long one commencing with a rich soup made of lamb's head and entrails known as mayeritsa. This is followed by olives, citrus fruits, the Paschal lamb or kid, red hard-boiled eggs – the colour symbolizes the blood of Christ – and many cheerful toasts and good resolutions, and last but not least, the egg-studded Easter Breads, Tsoureki, Pashkalina and Lambropsomo.

TSOUREKI (Greece)

60g (2oz) fresh yeast
⅛ litre (¼ pint) warm water
¼ litre (½ pint) warm milk
350g (12oz) sugar
1¼kg (3lb) flour
7 eggs

grated rind of one lemon
or 1 tablespoon ground
aniseed
1 cup melted butter
6–8 red hard-boiled eggs*

Dissolve the yeast in the water. Add the milk, one teaspoon of the sugar and two cups of the flour. Beat the mixture well with a wooden spoon, cover and prove till bubbly. Beat the eggs, the remaining sugar and lemon rind over hot water until light. Add the remaining flour to the eggs and then combine it with the yeast mixture. Knead the melted butter into the dough. Continue kneading till the dough is elastic and smooth. Gather into a ball, grease and place in a large bowl to prove till double in bulk. Divide into twelve equal parts. Shape the parts into ropes about 2½cm (1in) in diameter. Braid into four plaits, plunging one or more hard-boiled red eggs into each loaf. Cover and allow to prove. Brush with beaten egg and bake at 190°C/375°F for 25–30 minutes.

* To colour the eggs, boil them in water that has been tinted with food colouring or to which onion (brown or red) skins have been added.

LAMBROPSOMO (Greece)

¼ litre (½ pint) milk
40g (1½oz) fresh yeast
200g (7oz) sugar
125g (4½oz) butter
1 teaspoon salt

grated rind of 1 lemon
  or orange
4 eggs
1kg (2¼lb) flour
4 red hard-boiled eggs

Scald the milk, putting a quarter of it aside to cool to luke-warm. Dissolve the yeast and one teaspoon of sugar in the lukewarm milk. Place the butter, remaining sugar, salt and lemon rind in the remaining hot milk and let it cool to luke-warm. Combine the yeast and butter mixtures and stir in the lightly beaten eggs. Beat in the flour with a wooden spoon, using the hand to mix the dough when it becomes too stiff to beat. Gather into a ball and turn out on to a lightly floured board. Knead for 10 minutes, adjusting the amount of flour to make a soft but not sticky dough. Return the dough to a greased bowl, turning it to coat on all sides with grease. Cover and prove till double in bulk. Punch down the dough and knead lightly. Pinch off a fistful of dough and reserve. Form the bulk of the dough into a round loaf and place on a greased baking sheet. Divide the reserved dough into two parts and roll each into a rope the width of the loaf. Slash the ropes 10cm (4in) along their ends. Lay the strips cross-wise over the Lambropsomo, bending back the slashed ends. Press a red hard-boiled egg into each point of the cross where the ends curl, cover the loaf and prove till risen. Brush with beaten egg and bake at 190°C/375°F for 50–55 minutes.

COLOMBA DI PASQUA
Italian Dove of Easter

This bread, which is sold at Eastertime in Italy, is symbolic of much that is temporal and religious. In ancient times the dove represented fertility and thence peace, perhaps because of the very harmlessness of the creature. The Old Testament describes the return of the dove to Noah who was stranded in the Ark on Mount Ararat, bearing 'in her mouth an olive leaf pluckt off' (Genesis, ch. 8, v. 11), as proof of his salvation and the presence of dry land. Sacrifices of young doves were often made, and in ancient days as well as today, doves were kept in decorative cotes. At Christ's baptism the Holy Spirit assumed the form of a dove and fluttered over Jesus' head, betokening peace and innocence.

In Italy the bread therefore has great significance, and is exchanged between families and friends at Eastertime in remembrance of Christ's gentle nature, his death and subsequent joyful resurrection. I was once given a present of three Easter biscuits from Italy, which I kept for many years and finally threw out with great reluctance when they were past saving. One was of a camel, another of a lamb and the third and most interesting of a woman with three breasts. They were supposed to be fertility biscuits, the animals being sacrificial.

The loaves can be made as individual small birds or shaped to form one large dove.

milk
20g (⅔oz) fresh yeast
175g (6oz) sugar
125g (4½oz) butter
1 tablespoon grated lemon rind
2½ teaspoons vanilla essence
1 teaspoon salt
6 egg yolks
750g (1lb 11 oz) flour

Almond Paste
⅓ cup almond paste
2 tablespoons sugar
1 egg white

Glaze
1 egg white
¼ cup sliced almonds

Scald the milk, and pour $\frac{1}{4}$ cup of it into a small bowl and allow to cool to lukewarm. Crumble the yeast into this together with one teaspoon sugar, and stir till dissolved. Cover the bowl and allow to stand for 10 minutes. Meanwhile, combine the softened butter, sugar, lemon rind, vanilla and salt, and pour the remaining milk over the mixture. When this mixture is lukewarm add the yeast to it, and stir thoroughly. Now beat the egg yolks lightly and add them to the butter and milk mixture. Beat in enough flour to make a soft dough and turn it out on to a lightly floured board. Continue to knead the dough, adding the remaining flour, or enough to make an elastic but not sticky dough. Cover, and prove till double in bulk. Meanwhile make the almond paste: mix $\frac{1}{3}$ cup almond paste with an egg white and 2 tablespoons sugar. Punch down the dough and shape as follows: to make one large dove, divide the dough into two parts. Shape one part into an elongated oval and lay it across the breadth of a greased baking sheet. Form the other into a triangle with a narrow base and long sides and place it across the oval. Hold the triangle in the centre and twist it once, thereby forming the body of the dove. Pinch in the dough about 10cm (4in) from the tip of the triangle to form the neck and elongate the tip of the triangle to shape the beak. With the blunt edge of a knife score the tail and wings to simulate feathers. Place a caraway seed in the head section for an eye. Brush the scored parts with almond paste, and allow the dough to rise till light. Brush the surface of the dove with one egg white, and sprinkle with $\frac{1}{4}$ cup sliced almonds and 1 tablespoon sugar. Bake at 190°C/375°F for 40–45 minutes. Serve warm. To make several small doves, shape the dough after proving as follows: roll into ropes about the thickness of the finger and cut them into lengths of about 20cm (8in). Knot the lengths so as to leave the ends 5cm (2in) long. To form the tail, flatten one end and slash to simulate feathers. Round the other end to form the dove's head, pinching the dough at the end of the head to form a beak. Brush the doves with almond paste, prove and bake at 200°C/400°F for 15 minutes.

BRIOCHE EN COURONNE (France)

Brioche en Couronne is a special form of brioche which is made in the shape of a large ring or crown. In France during the Easter season pastry shops have enchanting displays of moulded ducks, lambs, and hens as well as the customary chocolate eggs. In pagan and early Christian times, animals were sacrificed at the altar, originally to give thanksgiving for the return of Spring and later as part of the Easter feast. In France it was customary for the lordly landowners to distribute Brioche en Couronne to the needy at Easter Mass.

Make one quantity of brioche dough as given under BRIOCHE À TÊTE (p. 109) and allow it to prove once. Punch down the dough and shape it into a ball. With the handle of a wooden spoon poke a hole through the middle of the ball and, lifting the dough into the air, gradually enlarge the ring by turning and moulding it. Place the brioche on a greased baking sheet and allow to prove till double in bulk. With scissors, clip around the outer and inner edges of the dough ring, making triangular points. Brush the brioche with beaten egg and bake at 190°C/375°F for 30–35 minutes.

PÄÄSIÄISLEIPÄ
Finnish Easter Bread

Finnish housewives delight in turning out wholesome breads. This holiday loaf is traditionally baked in a milk pail to symbolize the spring abundance of dairy foods and the birth of new calves. Filled with filberts and raisins, the bread resembles an overgrown mushroom when turned out of the pail. New season strawberries, sweet butter and cheeses such as Camembert and Brie make ideal accompaniments.

40g (1½oz) fresh yeast
¼ cup lukewarm water
1½ cups single cream,
    scalded and cooled
2 cups strong plain flour
5 egg yolks
1 cup sugar
250g (9oz) melted butter,
    cooled
1½ teaspoons salt
2 teaspoons ground
    cardamom

1 cup chopped filberts
    or almonds
2 teaspoons grated lemon
    peel
2 tablespoons grated orange
    peel
1 cup raisins
1 cup scalded and cooled
    milk
2 cups rye flour
4–4½ cups strong plain flour

Dissolve yeast in the lukewarm water in a bowl. Stir in the cream and 2 cups of flour. Beat vigorously till the mixture is smooth. Cover the bowl and allow the dough to prove till doubled in bulk. Stir in the egg yolks, sugar, butter, salt, cardamom, nuts, lemon peel, orange peel and raisins, and beat until thoroughly combined. Add the milk and rye flour and stir till combined. Next stir in the remaining plain flour and knead with the hands in the bowl to make a rough dough. Turn out on to a floured board and knead firmly for 10 minutes. Return the dough to the greased bowl, turning it in the bowl to coat all sides with grease. Cover, and prove till double in bulk. Punch down the dough, knead lightly, and place in a straight sided 4 litre (7 pint) pail. Alternatively, the dough can be divided between two smaller pails. Bake at 175°C/350°F for about 1½ hours till done: as the loaf is very large it will be necessary to test it with a skewer to see whether the middle of the bread is cooked. Brush the top of the loaf with melted butter.

HOT CROSS BUNS

Traditionally baked and served on Good Friday, warm and spicy Hot Cross Buns have distinct religious and mythological origins. The familiar cross-shaped markings can be traced far back to pre-Christian times in such cities as Babylon and in Egypt as well. The cross represented both sun and fire, the sun symbol being a circle bisected by two lines into four quarters, which represented the four seasons. Both the Greeks and the Romans had festive cakes which bore such symbols. Other loaves were marked with yet another powerful fire-sun symbol that was later christianized: a central disc like a wheel. Roman bread so marked has been found under the preservative volcanic ash in the ruins of Herculaneum. The buns as we know them today were popularized in the thirteenth century as a gift for family and friends on Good Friday, and for those who had far to travel before reaching church on Easter Sunday. The nursery rhyme of 1797 seems to have a different use for them however:

'Hot cross buns! Hot cross buns!
One a penny, two a penny, hot cross buns.
If you have no daughters, leave them to your sons,
One a penny, two a penny
Hot cross buns!'

To make 20 buns

6 *tablespoons milk*	¼ *litre (½ pint) milk*
25g *(1oz) fresh yeast*	2 *eggs*
450g *(1lb) flour*	60g *(2oz) sweet butter,*
¼ *teaspoon allspice*	*softened*
1 *teaspoon ground cinnamon*	60g *(2oz) sultanas*
½ *teaspoon salt*	1 *lightly beaten egg mixed with*
5 *teaspoons sugar*	2½ *teaspoons double cream*

Warm the 6 tablespoons milk to lukewarm and dissolve the yeast in it. Cover the yeast mixture and stand it in a warm place to prove for 5 to 8 minutes. Sift the flour, spices, salt and sugar into a large bowl. Press a well into the centre of the flour and pour the yeast and milk mixture into it. Add the remaining milk together with the eggs, and beat vigorously with a wooden spoon till bubbles appear on the surface of the dough. Add three-quarters of the butter in small pieces, turn out on to a floured board and knead in more flour till the dough has taken up enough to be soft and easily handled. Continue kneading till the dough is silky to the touch. Gather into a ball and place in a greased bowl, rotating the dough so that all its surfaces are coated with grease. Prove till double in bulk, then punch down and lift on to a floured board. Lightly knead the dough, incorporating the sultanas into the mixture. Pinch off a small amount of dough and reserve it for making the crosses. Divide the remaining dough into 20 equal pieces and fashion into buns. Place the buns on greased baking sheets and slash a cross on each bun. Roll the reserved dough into thin strips and lay two strips across each bun in the form of a cross. Allow to prove briefly, brush with the beaten egg and cream. Bake at 200°C/400°F for 15–20 minutes until golden.

BAYERISCHE ÖSTERMÄNNLEIN (Germany)

These Easter men are natives of Bavaria and are given to children as presents at Eastertime. The eggs which they cradle in their arms can be coloured by adding food colouring to the water in which they are boiled prior to baking.

500g (1lb 2oz) flour
25g (1oz) fresh yeast
75g (2½oz) sugar
⅛ litre (¼ pint) milk
75g (2½oz) butter

½ teaspoon salt
grated peel of 1 lemon
1 egg yolk
8 small hard-boiled eggs

Sift the flour into a large mixing bowl. Press a well into the centre of the flour and crumble the yeast into it. Add one teaspoon of sugar and a little lukewarm milk to the yeast and stir to make a paste, drawing a little flour in from the edges of the well as you do so. Cover the bowl and allow to prove

for about 25 minutes. Add all the other ingredients, except
the egg yolk and eggs, and beat briskly with a wooden spoon,
or in an electric mixer set at a slow speed till all ingredients
are well combined and the dough starts to throw bubbles on
its surface and leaves the sides of the bowl. Divide the dough
into eight portions and shape each part into a man with
hands clasped in front of the body. Transfer the Easter men
to greased baking sheets and then place a hard-boiled and
coloured egg in their arms. Form the face with the help of
currants for eyes and orange peel or angelica for nose and
mouth. Allow to prove for 20 minutes or till puffed, brush
with the beaten egg yolk and bake at 200°C/400°F for 20–30
minutes until golden.

SACRIFICIAL SUN SHAPES

The symbol of the circle is one of the oldest shapes known to
man. Long before the birth of Christ and civilization as we
know it today man worshipped the sun and the rhythm of
the seasons, and paid homage to gods long since forgotten. I
would like to be able to introduce the following cakes under
the title of 'Stonehenge Cookies' but as the Celts probably
ate unleavened bread that would most likely be erroneous.
The ancient shape, however, is known to have represented
the sun and its miraculous return after the long winter
months. It was later taken over by the Christians who used
the form to symbolize Easter. Cakes such as these can still
be bought at Eastertime in some southern parts of Central
Europe.

500g (1 lb 2oz) flour	125g (4½oz) butter
25g (1oz) yeast	1 teaspoon salt
100g (4oz) sugar	vanilla
4 tablespoons milk	1 beaten egg
2 tablespoons rum	vanilla icing
1 large egg	

Sift the flour into a large bowl and press a well into the centre. Crumble the yeast into the well and add one teaspoon sugar and half the lukewarm milk. Stir the milk and yeast, drawing in a little flour from the sides of the well to make a paste. Cover the bowl and allow the yeast sponge to become bubbly. Add the rest of the milk, the rum, egg, warmed but not melted butter, sugar, salt and vanilla, and beat vigorously till the dough leaves the sides of the bowl and throws bubbles. Dust the dough ball lightly, return it to the bowl and prove till double in bulk. Form the dough into ropes by dividing it into manageable pieces and rolling them firmly on a floured working surface. The sun shapes can be formed in the shape of a cartwheel with slashed edges; by crossing two ropes of dough and curling the ends; or, by interlocking two circles and pulling them in opposing directions and thereby shaping an ellipse. Place the suns on greased baking sheets, cover them and allow to prove till light and puffy. Brush with beaten egg. Bake at 190–200°C/ 375–400°F for 20 minutes. Allow to cool slightly, then brush with vanilla icing.

Christmas Breads

DRESDNER CHRISTSTOLLEN (Germany)

Traditional and beloved fare of the German Christmas-tide, the Christstollen is to be found on every table from Christmas Eve until well after the Twelve Days of Christmas have elapsed. The symbolic folding of the dough prior to baking represents the swaddling of the Christ child in his bands. In many households as many as 12 Stollen are baked, in which case the risen loaves are carried on trays to the local baker who then bakes them in his roomy oven. I well remember my father-in-law being called on to knead some ten pounds of flour once – the rest of the family watched with interest as his bared and powerful forearms quickly kneaded the dough to exactly the right consistency.

There are many varieties of Stollen but the Dresdner one is generally regarded as being everyman's favourite.

1kg (2¼lb) flour
100g (4oz) fresh yeast
200g (7oz) sugar
½ litre (1 pint) milk
10g (⅓oz) salt
½ teaspoon cardamom
½ teaspoon mace
grated rind of one lemon
500g (1lb 2oz) raisins
150g (5oz) currants

250g (9oz) chopped mixed peel
150g (5oz) chopped sweet almonds
30g (1oz) chopped bitter almonds

Glaze
100g (4oz) butter
sugar crystals or icing

Place the sifted flour into a large bowl and press a well into the centre. Crumble the yeast and place it in the well together with 2 teaspoons sugar. Pour a little warm milk over the yeast and sugar, mixing it to make a paste with some of the flour from the sides of the well. Cover the bowl and allow the yeast to 'sponge' in a warm place for about 40 minutes. Add the rest of the milk, the melted but not hot butter, salt, spices, sugar and grated lemon peel. Beat the mixture vigorously with a wooden spoon till the dough shows bubbles under its surface. Now add the fruits and nuts and knead the dough till it is elastic. Gather into a ball and prove till double in volume. Knead lightly a second time and again allow to prove. Divide the dough into two or three portions and form it into Stollen. Roll the dough out, mark it into thirds and fold over first one third and then the other. Gently run fingers along the join to secure it, though it should remain noticeable. Place the Stollen on greased baking sheets and prove for a further 30 minutes. Bake at 180 to 200°C/350 to 400°F for 70–90 minutes till golden and done. Cover with foil if browning is too rapid. While hot, brush with melted butter and glaze with icing or sugar crystals.

PANETTONE DI NATALE (Italy)

20g (⅔oz) fresh yeast
100g (4oz) sugar
2 tablespoons warm water
750g (1lb 11oz) flour
175g (6oz) butter
3 eggs
2 egg yolks
a little warm milk
1 teaspoon vanilla essence

75g (2½oz) chopped
  candied lemon peel
75g (2½oz) chopped
  candied orange peel
⅓ cup raisins
75g (2½oz) chopped,
  blanched almonds
whole blanched almonds
  for decoration

Dissolve the yeast together with one teaspoon sugar in the warm water, cover, and allow to stand for ten minutes. Sift the flour into a large bowl and press a well into the centre. Pour the yeast into the centre, and stir to make a paste. Cover and allow to rest a little. Cream the butter and sugar and add the eggs and egg yolks. Combine the warm milk and the eggs and butter mixture with the yeast paste and vanilla, and, with the hand, work the ingredients together to form a dough. Turn out on to a floured board and knead for five minutes. Divide the dough into two equal parts and into one part knead the fruits and almonds. Grease both dough balls, cover and prove till double in bulk. Roll out each amount of dough to a long triangle of the same size. Place one on top of the other and roll up to form a sausage starting from the base of the triangle. Grease a tube or loaf pan, sprinkle with sugar and stud with whole blanched almonds. Place the roll inside the pan and set to prove. The dough should come about two-thirds up the sides of the pan. If the pan seems too short, tie a greased paper collar around the free end to allow for rising. Prove. Bake at 200°C/400°F for 10 minutes, then decrease the temperature to 190°C/375°F and bake a further 50 minutes or till done.

TWELTH CAKES

'Heaped up on the floor, to form a kind of throne, were
turkeys, geese, game, poultry, wreaths of sausages, mince
pies, plum puddings, barrels of oysters, red-hot chest-
nuts, cherry-cheeked apples, juicy oranges, luscious
pears, immense twelth cakes, and seething bowls of
punch, that made the chamber dim with their steam
... Scrooge ... came peeping round the door.'

A Christmas Carol CHARLES DICKENS

This steaming fragrant 'cake' baked in celebration of Twelth
Night, or Epiphany, when the three magi, Caspar, Melchior
and Balthazar were led by the Star of Bethlehem to the crib
of Jesus, is virtually unknown today. In Dickens's time, however, it was still popular and a traditional part of the Christmas festival. The recipe which follows is a nineteenth cen-
tuary interpretation of an early seventeenth century one –
the ingredients are therefore given in generous proportions.

1kg (2lb) butter	1kg (2lb) flour
1kg (2lb) loaf sugar	2 kg (4lb) currants
1 nutmeg, ground	½kg (1lb) chopped candied
7½g (¼oz) ginger	lemon peel
a little mixed spice	¼kg (½lb) chopped candied
20 eggs	orange peel
1 wine-glass brandy	¼kg (½lb) almonds

Work the butter to a smooth cream with the hand, mix it
with the pounded loaf sugar and the spices and work them
well together for ten minutes. Then break in the eggs gradually and beat it for twenty minutes. Add the brandy, then
the flour, again stirring well together; add the currants
washed and dried, and the candied peel cut into shreds, and
the almonds blanched and chopped very fine. Mix very
thoroughly and put into a hoop lined with buttered paper;

smooth it on top with your hand dipped in milk, and put the hoop on a baking sheet, and then a raised stand in the oven to prevent the bottom of the cake from burning and bake it for 4½ hours in a slow oven. When nearly cold, ice it all over and decorate it with fancy articles of any description, with a high ornament in the centre.

LUCIA BUNS (Sweden)

'Ut filiae lucis ambulate' (Walk as daughters of the light). In Sweden the celebration of the Feast of Saint Lucia falls on December 13 and marks the opening of the Christmas season. Each year the daughter of the house dons a white robe girded by a red belt, and bearing a pine wreath lit by candles on her head, she brings each occupant of the house saffron cakes. Her passage through the house is accompanied by her own singing, and each recipient of her Lucia buns is serenaded as well.

2 tablespoons boiling water
1 teaspoon crushed saffron
¼ litre (½ pint) milk
30g (1oz) fresh yeast
85g (3oz) sugar
½ teaspoon salt

125g (4½oz) butter
650g (1lb 7oz) flour
1 egg
raisins for decoration
1 lightly beaten egg white
coarse sugar

Pour the 2 tablespoons of boiling water over the saffron and leave to soak for 30 minutes. Scald the milk and pour a little of it into a small bowl. Allow it to cool to lukewarm and dissolve the yeast and one teaspoon sugar in it. Stir the salt, sugar and softened butter into the remaining milk. Combine the yeast mixture with the butter mixture and beat in a third of the flour to make a batter. Sieve the saffron liquid into the batter, pressing the saffron grounds to expel all the colour. Lightly beat the egg and add it to the batter. Gradually beat in the remaining flour, working with the hand when the dough becomes too stiff to beat. Turn out on to a floured board and knead, adjusting the amount of flour to give a very soft but not sticky dough. Cover and prove till double in bulk. Punch down the dough and divide it into 36 equal parts. Roll each part into a rope the length of a handspan. Shape each rope into a 'C' with the ends curling inwards and place them in pairs back to back on a greased baking sheet. Place a raisin at the centre of each coil, cover and prove till light and puffy. Brush with beaten egg white and sprinkle with coarse sugar. Bake at 200°C/400°F for 15–20 minutes.

CHRISTMAS POINSETTIA STAR

In northern hemisphere countries the poinsettia is known as the 'Christmas Star' and can be bought in pots at Christmas time, for which it is very popular as it blooms for a very long period, and with a little persuasion and expertise on the part of its owner can be brought to flower again the following year. Countries in the southern hemisphere, however, enjoy their Christmas in mid-summer, and the poinsettia in mid-winter at which time the flower is blooming everywhere – in hedges and trees, but rarely in pots.

This loaf is ideal for Christmas as its shape represents the Star which guided the Wise Men to Bethlehem. The plaiting requires practice, so try it out before you start making the loaf.

800g (1lb 12oz) flour	1 egg
30g (1oz) fresh yeast	1 egg yolk
¼ litre (½ pint) milk	1 tablespoon lard
70g (2½oz) sugar	125g (4½oz) mixed peel and
150g (5oz) butter	currants
1 teaspoon salt	

Sift and halve the flour. Place one half in a large bowl, press a well in the centre, and into this well crumble the yeast.

Add a little of the lukewarm milk and one teaspoon of the sugar, and stir to make a paste, drawing in a little of the flour from the sides of the well. Cover the bowl and prove for 15 minutes. Meanwhile, mix the remaining ingredients with the other half of the flour to make a smooth dough. Combine both mixtures and knead for 5 minutes. Cover and prove till double in bulk. Divide the dough into 12 equal parts and roll each part into a rope of finger thickness. Group the ropes in four and plait each group to half its length. Place the plaits on a greased baking sheet in the following way: divide the four unplaited ropes into twos and fold down the side of the plaited part. Place three pieces of dough shaped like this on the baking sheet, evenly spaced, with the free ends facing out. Now, taking two strands from each neighbouring group, plait a new strand of four, working to the outside of the star. Continue in this way until all strands are plaited. Prove again briefly, and brush with egg yolk. Bake at 200°C/400°F for 20 minutes till golden.

JULEKAKE
Scandinavian Christmas Bun

A most economical, large fruit bun with butter to keep it moist and fresh for days.

100g (4oz) butter	1 egg
500g (1lb 2oz) flour	100g (4oz) raisins or
100g (4oz) sugar	sultanas
1 level teaspoon cardamom	100g (4oz) candied peel
¼ litre (½ pint) milk	1 teaspoon lemon rind
50g (2oz) fresh yeast	1 beaten egg for the glaze

Rub the butter into the flour and fold in the sugar and cardamom. Warm the milk to lukewarm and dissolve the yeast in it. Mix in the lightly beaten egg. Gradually add the milk and egg to the flour and work well to make a dough; mix in the fruit and peel. Prove till double in bulk. Work the risen dough well on a floured surface then shape into two round cakes, being careful to avoid cracking the dough. Place the cakes on greased baking sheets and allow to rise till double in bulk again. Make a hole through the centre of each loaf with a wooden spoon to prevent the dough from cracking during baking. Brush with beaten egg and cook at 200°C/400°F for 15–20 minutes till golden.

This same dough can be used to make *Kringele* or *Stangen*, in which case the dough is rolled out in the shape of a rectangle. To form a *Stange* it is rolled into a stick along the long edge – in the same way in which French bread is prepared. *Kringele* means ring, and hence the dough is rolled up in the same fashion, the ends being pinched together to form a circle. After being allowed to prove, these loaves are brushed with beaten egg and sprinkled lavishly with chopped almonds and coarse sugar mixed with cinnamon.

BISHOP'S BREAD (Germany)

This is a delicious Christmas bread fit not only for bishops but for kings as well. Traditionally baked in a 'Rehrücken' or log baking form, the Bishop's Bread is best eaten after it has aged for a day or two. It also makes good toast.

¼ cup raisins	pinch salt
3 tablespoons dark rum	175g (6oz) castor sugar
200g (7oz) butter	500g (1lb 2oz) flour
125g (4½oz) icing sugar	2 teaspoons baking powder
grated rind of one lemon	1 cup chopped mixed peel
½ teaspoon vanilla essence	1 cup chopped walnuts
7 eggs	⅓ cup chocolate bits

Soak the raisins in the rum overnight. Cream the butter and icing sugar till fluffy; add the lemon rind and vanilla. Separate the eggs and add the yolks one at a time. In another bowl

beat the egg whites with the salt till they hold soft peaks and
then slowly beat in the castor sugar. Continue beating the
whites till they are stiff. Fold the egg whites gently into the
yolk and butter mixture, and then fold in the sifted flour and
baking powder. Now add the peel, walnuts, raisins and
chocolate bits. Grease a baking form and sprinkle fine breadcrumbs over its surface. Pour the batter into the form and
spread it evenly with a spatula. Bake at 200°C/400°F for 10
minutes, then reduce the temperature to 180°C/350°F and
bake a further 40–50 minutes. Let the bread cool for a while
in the form before turning out.

MÁKOS ÉS DIÓS KALÁCS
Hungarian Christmas Bread

This bread is similar to the Christmas breads of Austria and
Bavaria. It is unmistakably Continental in that it contains a
filling of sweetened poppy-seeds – these are much cheaper if
bought in bulk from a health food store. Try serving it at
Christmas time as an alternative to our fruited cake.

Dough	Filling
¼ litre (½ pint) lukewarm milk	250g (9oz) poppy-seeds
30g (1oz) fresh yeast	60g (2oz) almonds
125g (4½oz) sugar	1 egg
150–200g (5–7oz) butter	100g (4oz) sugar
¼ teaspoon salt	vanilla essence
2 eggs	45g (1½oz) flour
grated rind of ½ lemon	60g (2oz) sultanas
750g (1lb 11oz) flour	7½g (¼oz) fresh yeast
	vanilla icing for glazing

Heat the milk to lukewarm. Crumble the yeast into the milk,
together with one teaspoon of the sugar. Stir to dissolve.
Cover and let stand for 10 minutes. Combine the butter,
sugar, salt, eggs and lemon rind in a bowl, then gradually

add the flour alternately with the yeast mixture. Work the dough with the hand then turn out on to a floured board and knead till smooth and elastic. Roll the dough into a ball and grease lightly. Cover and prove till double in bulk. Meanwhile, prepare the filling: boil the poppy-seeds gently for 30 minutes in 1 litre (2 pints) of water. Drain and pour another litre (2 pints) of cold water over the poppy-seeds – this takes away their bitterness. After 10 minutes, drain the seeds and grind in a coffee grinder. Mix with the other filling ingredients, except the yeast, and bring to the boil once. Let the filling cool to lukewarm and then stir in the dissolved yeast. Punch down the dough and knead lightly. Roll out to two large rectangles and divide the filling between each. Spread over the dough then roll up starting at the long side. Place the rolls on separate greased trays and prove till well risen. Bake at 200°C/400°F for 50–55 minutes. While still warm brush with a little vanilla icing or melted butter.

SWISS CHRISTMAS PEAR BREAD

This Christmas bread comes from the town of Glarus in the Glarner Alps and is unusual in that it contains dried pears and plums.

500g (1lb 2oz) dried pears	⅛ teaspoon ground cloves
200g (7oz) stoned, dried plums	1 tablespoon kirsch
100g (4oz) raisins	300g (11oz) flour
100g (4oz) figs	½ cup milk
50g (2oz) candied lemon peel	50g (2oz) butter
150g (5oz) chopped walnuts	15g (½oz) fresh yeast
⅛ teaspoon cinnamon	1 egg
	½ teaspoon salt
	egg for glaze

Soak the pears and plums overnight and simmer them in a little water and sugar till they are soft. Drain the pears and plums and force them through a sieve. Mix the purée with the other fruits, walnuts, spices and kirsch and put it to one side.

To make the bread dough: sift the flour into a large bowl and press a well into the centre. Heat the milk till it is luke-warm and drop the butter, cut into small pieces, into it. Dissolve the yeast in the milk, cover, and allow to stand for 10 minutes. Pour the yeast mixture into the well in the flour, and break the egg into it. Scatter the salt over the flour, then, using a whisk, beat the ingredients to combine them. When the dough becomes too stiff to work with the whisk, use the hand to combine the ingredients further. Turn the dough out on to a floured surface and knead till it is elastic. Cover and prove till double in bulk. Roll the dough out to the shape of a rectangle and spoon the fruit and spice mixture over one half. Fold the other half over the fruit, pressing the edges firmly together. Gently press the roll together, cover, and prove for 30–45 minutes. Brush the pear bread with beaten egg, prick it all over with a fork, and bake at 190°C/375°F for 10 minutes, reducing the heat to 180°C/350°F for a further 40–50 minutes.

GINGER CHOCOLATE HEARTS (Germany)

These German gingerbread hearts can be made well before Christmas and are often used to decorate the Christmas tree. They are commonly eaten on the four Advents leading up to Christmas Day. On each successive Advent Sunday, first one, then two, then three and finally four candles are lit and either placed in candle holders on the tea table, or amongst the branches of a pine wreath which is suspended from the ceiling by four red ribbons.

125g (4½oz) ground
  hazelnuts
125g (4½oz) ground almonds
250g (9oz) icing sugar

1 tablespoon honey
60g (2oz) finely chopped
  crystallized orange peel
2 egg whites

½ teaspoon ground ginger
¼ teaspoon cinnamon
¼ teaspoon cardamom

rice wafers for base
1 teaspoon butter
150g (5oz) chocolate

Mix the nuts, icing sugar, honey and chopped orange peel.
Beat the egg whites till they hold stiff peaks and then fold
the spices into them. Combine the two mixtures thoroughly
and then roll out on a board which has been generously
sprinkled with sugar. The dough should be 8mm (⅓in) thick.
Stamp out heart-shaped forms with a biscuit cutter, dipping
the cutter in sugar each time, and transfer each form carefully to a wafer. If the wafers are round, the excess wafer can
be broken off after baking. Bake at 180°C/350°F for 20–25
minutes. When done, transfer the hearts to a rack to cool.
Melt the butter and chocolate together over a low heat. If
the icing seems too thick, add a little hot water. With a
kitchen skewer, bore a hole through the heart and thread
with ribbon.

Dip each heart in the chocolate icing and hang on a stick
till dry.

Other Festive Breads

GINGERBREAD MEN

'Run, run as fast as you can,
You can't catch me
I'm the gingerbread man!'

Gingerbread is considered by many to be a cake, but it was
originally meant to be served as a bread – as the name im-
plies – at lunch or dinner. Associations such as Tiddy Dolls
and the childhood delight of a slow and delicious dismember-

ment of the gingerbread man's parts keep the memory of his brief existence very much alive.

1 *cup golden syrup*	100g *(4oz) brown sugar*
100g *(4oz) butter*	1½ *teaspoons ground ginger*
1 *teaspoon bicarbonate of soda*	250g *(9oz) flour*

Melt the golden syrup and butter together in a saucepan. Allow the mixture to cool a little, then add the bicarbonate of soda, sugar and spice. Sift the flour into the mixture and work to a stiff paste. Roll out the dough on a floured board and cut out men by hand or use a special cutter. Using currants, almonds and crystallized peel for decoration, form the eyes, nose and mouth of the gingerbread men. Bake till golden at 180°C/350°F for 15–20 minutes. Transfer to a rack to cool. Fit a writing nozzle on an icing gun and decorate the men with vanilla icing.

MARTINMAS HORSESHOES

These delicious leavened pastries commemorate St Martin, the pious Bishop of Tours who lived in the fourth century. He was a much loved patron of the early church, responsible for the spreading of Christianity amongst a Europe which was still largely under Roman occupation. To this day some 3,675 churches and 425 villages in France bear his name, and in the Hungarian town of Szombothely where he met his death, Martinmas on November 11 is of particular importance. The pastries are made in the shape of a horseshoe and studded with currants for 'nails' in remembrance of the saint who never tired of travelling to serve the Church.

As the dough is a variation on puff pastry, adequate time must be allowed between tours, so be sure to prepare the dough half a day before it is needed.

Dough

500g (1lb 2oz) flour
⅛ litre (¼ pint) milk
40g (1½oz) fresh yeast
60g (2oz) sugar
200g (7oz) butter
1 egg
1 teaspoon salt
grated rind of one lemon
1 egg white

1 egg yolk
100g (4oz) currants

Filling

125g (4½oz) marzipan
60g (2oz) butter
2 egg yolks
85g (3oz) sugar
few drops vanilla essence
100g (4oz) flour

Sift the flour into a large bowl and press a well into the centre. Heat the milk to lukewarm and dissolve the yeast and 1 teaspoon sugar in it. Pour the yeast and milk into the well and stir to form a paste with some of the flour. Cover and allow to stand for 10 minutes. Next add 60g (2oz) soft, but not melted, butter, egg, salt, remaining sugar and lemon and beat the dough till it leaves the sides of the bowl and bubbles appear under its surface. Gather the dough into a ball, dust it with flour and leave in the bowl to prove for about 30 minutes. Roll out 140g (5oz) butter between two pieces of waxed paper to a rectangle measuring 25 × 40cm (10 × 16in), and return it to the refrigerator to become firm. Roll out the dough to a rectangle measuring 40 × 50cm (16 × 20in), and place the cooled slab of butter in the middle. Fold the left and right dough flaps over the butter, press the edges together to seal the envelope and, with a rolling pin, make corrugations down the length of the dough. Rolling in one direction only, roll out the dough to form a band about 50cm (20in) long. Fold the short edges of the band towards the centre, and fold again once. Place the dough 'packet' in the refrigerator to cool for 15 minutes. This is known as one 'tour'. Repeat the tours three times, but subsequently only fold the dough in three parts instead of four. During this time, make the filling by mixing the ingredients to a paste, adding the flour gradually. Roll out the dough to a thickness of 1cm (½in) and cut it into rectangles measuring

6 × 12cm (2½ × 5in). Place a little filling along one side of the rectangle, fold the other side over it and seal the edges with egg white. Press the edges firmly together, rotate the seam to the underside and bend the pastries into a horseshoe shape. Prove briefly till puffy, brush with beaten egg yolk and bake at 200°C/400°F for 15–20 minutes. Brush with vanilla icing while still warm and stud with currants.

SCHINKEN IM BROTTEIG
Ham in Bread (Germany)

JAMBON AU BOURGONNE EN CROÛTE
Ham in Bread (France)

The method of roasting meat whereby it is encased in dough is one which has been practised since the dawn of culinary history. Originally, the dough case served only to protect the meat during cooking and was later cracked and discarded. In the Middle Ages bread was even baked in flat ovals known as 'trenchers' to serve as plates which were eaten with the meal or thrown to the poor at the end of the feast – thence 'good trencherman', meaning one who could eat vast quantities of food at one sitting.

I have grouped these two recipes together because they are both very popular as festive dishes in the countries of their origin. The French recipe uses a dough which is leavened by the inclusion of baking powder; the German recipe features a sour dough rye crust.

SCHINKEN IM BROTTEIG Select a lightly smoked ham, preferably Westphalian Ham, and have the butcher bone it. Some country hams require boiling before baking in the oven, in which case soak the ham overnight and scrub it before the boiling starts. Simmer the ham for 18–20 minutes per 450g (1lb), and allow it to drain thoroughly. Place it fatty side up on a trivet in a covered roasting pan. Pour enough cider or apfelsaft into the pan to measure 5cm

(2½in) in depth. Roast the meat in a moderate oven allowing 30 minutes per 450g (1lb), basting it frequently with the juices. An hour before the cooking is completed, add a cup of sour or Morello cherry juice to the pan juices, and sprinkle the ham lightly with brown sugar. Douse the meat with ½ cup brandy and continue baking till done.

Have 1–1¼kg (2–3lb) of proved rye sour dough ready (scc Oberbayrisches Bauernbrot, page 98). Lift the cooked ham carefully from the pan and allow it to cool a little. Slice the ham into serving slices and reform into a ham shape. Roll out the dough to a large rectangle and drape it over the meat, sealing the edges by pinching them firmly together under the ham. Brush the Schinken with beaten egg, place it in a clean, greased roasting pan and bake it at 220°C/425°F till the crust is golden.

JAMBON AU BOURGONNE EN CROÛTE Select a lightly smoked ham and have the butcher bone it. Scrub the ham and soak it overnight in cold water. Place it in a large saucepan and cover with fresh water. Add a teaspoon of bruised peppercorns and bring the water to the boil. Simmer for 1½ hours, adding more water if necessary. Allow the ham to cool in its own liquid and then drain and sponge dry. Remove all the fat bar a layer of about 1cm (½in). Place the ham in a deep roasting pan and pour ¼litre (½pint) of burgundy over it. Bake at 180°C/350°F allowing 15–20 minutes per 450g (1lb), basting frequently with the pan juices. Lift the ham on to a carving board and slice thinly. Reshape the ham and brush it with a mixture of honey and the pan juices.

Prepare the following dough:

750g (1lb 11oz) flour	¼ teaspoon sage
3½ teaspoons baking powder	¼ teaspoon ground juniper berries
1½ teaspoons salt	250g (9oz) lard
¾ teaspoon mustard powder	¼ litre (½ pint) cold milk

Sift the dry ingredients together twice to ensure that the baking powder is evenly distributed through the flour. Cut in the lard and gradually add the cold milk, working quickly so that the dough does not become warm. Knead lightly and allow the dough to stand for 20 minutes. Roll out to a large rectangle and drape over the ham, tucking the edges under the meat. Cut a vent in the dome of the Jambon so that steam can escape during baking. Decorate with strips of dough and place the Jambon on a large greased baking sheet. Brush with cold milk before and during baking. Bake at 220°C/425°F for 15 minutes then lower the temperature to 190°C/375°F and bake a further 15 minutes or until the crust is golden. The Jambon en Croûte can be served hot or cold. If served cold, serve with a compôte of cranberries, Cumberland sauce, or apple sauce and horseradish. If served hot, prepare a sauce from the pan juices, adding a little burgundy for bouquet.

VASSILOPITTA
Greek New Year's Eve Bread

This bread is prepared for New Year's Eve and served at midnight, rather in the manner in which Hogmanay sees the passing of the Haggis. A gold or silver coin is hidden in the loaf, and upon serving, the person who receives the coin is said to have a year of good luck in store for him.

30g (1oz) fresh yeast	1 teaspoon salt
200ml (⅓ pint) warm milk	grated rind of one lemon
600g (1lb 5oz) flour	125g (4½oz) melted butter
200g (7oz) sugar	1 egg for the glaze
4 eggs	sesame seeds

Dissolve the yeast in the warm milk. Add a third of the flour and one teaspoon of the sugar and beat vigorously till the batter is smooth. Cover and prove till bubbly. Beat the eggs, sugar, salt and lemon rind over hot water and stir into the batter. Add the remaining flour, working with the hand. Gather the dough into a ball and turn out on to a lightly floured board. Knead, gradually adding the melted butter, until smooth and elastic. Cover and prove till double in bulk. Punch down the dough and knead lightly once again. Put in a buttered deep round baking dish. Cover and prove till double in bulk. Brush with lightly beaten egg and sprinkle with sesame seeds or almonds. Bake at 190°C/375°F for 40–45 minutes. When cold, pierce the loaf from underneath and insert a silver or gold coin deep into the bread.

PIED PIPER RATS

'Hamelin town's in Brunswick
By famous Hannover city. . . .'

. . . and thereby hangs quite a tale, immortalized for English speakers by the imaginative poet Browning, and for the residents of the township of Hammeln by the dogged interest and questioning of the tourist in their town. These yeasty rats have the Piper to thank for their existance – perhaps he even had them in mind when he put his pipe to his lips.

500g (1lb 2oz) flour	salt
⅛ litre (¼ pint) milk	10g (⅓oz) butter
⅛ litre (¼ pint) water	1 beaten egg
30g (1oz) fresh yeast	caraway seeds

Sift the flour into a large bowl and stand it in a warm but not hot oven. Scald the milk and add the water to it. Crumble the yeast into the milk and water and allow to stand a little. Press a well into the centre of the flour and pour the milk and yeast into it. Sprinkle about 1 teaspoon of salt around the outside edge of the flour, and then beat the mixture vigorously with a wooden spoon. Gather the dough into a ball, brush lightly with lukewarm water and allow to prove till double in bulk. Punch down the dough and knead it lightly. Shape into about 12 rats. To make the rat take a piece of dough and shape into a tapered cylinder. Pinch off a little dough and roll it into a long thin tail. Press the tail firmly on to the wide end of the cylinder. Make two circular slits slantways into the dough to form the ears, easing them gently away from the body. Place the rats on greased baking sheets and brush them sparingly with melted butter. Prove till double in bulk. Brush with beaten egg, and press caraway seeds into the head to form eyes, and, using almond slivers make two teeth at the end of the nose. Bake at 200°C/400°F for 15–20 minutes.

CHALLAH (Jewish)

Challah is a traditional braided Jewish loaf which is eaten on the Sabbath. The seven strands of dough which constitute the double plait of the Challah represent the days of the week, the 'Sabbath', or seventh strand being that which is intertwined through the other six. This bread is very light in texture, and tastes best when eaten warm, portions being torn from the loaf rather than cut.

25g (1oz) fresh yeast	$\frac{1}{4}$ litre ($\frac{1}{2}$ pint) oil
175ml ($\frac{1}{4}$ pint) honey	
3$\frac{1}{2}$ teaspoons salt	For glaze
400ml ($\frac{2}{3}$ pint) hot water	1 egg
1kg (2$\frac{1}{4}$lb) flour	poppyseeds
3 eggs	

In a large bowl combine the yeast, honey, salt and hot water. Add about one quarter of the flour and beat the mixture vigorously with a wooden spoon. Cover and allow to stand in a warm place for 20 minutes. Now add the beaten eggs and oil and stir till combined. Gradually add the remaining flour and more if necessary to make a soft dough. Continue working with the hand in the bowl till the ingredients are well combined. Gather the dough into a ball, and turn it out on to a floured board. Knead for about 10 minutes, grease the dough ball and return it to the bowl to prove till two fingermarks made in the dough remain after testing. It is important that the challah rises to the full on the first proving. Punch down the dough and knead lightly. Divide the dough into two equal parts, and from one half pinch off one-third of the dough and reserve. Fashion two plaits out of the two parts of dough, and place the smaller atop the larger. Next, roll out the reserved piece of dough to form a long rope, and either twine it between the two braids or, if you wish to bend the challah into a wreath shape, use it to make a decorative knot around the free ends.

Carefully lift the challah on to a very large greased baking sheet, cover and prove till fully double in bulk. Brush with beaten egg and scatter liberally with poppyseeds. Bake at 190°C/375°F, reducing the temperature to 180°C/350°F if the loaf browns too quickly, for 40–45 minutes.

Chapter Three

'THE BAKER'S DOZEN'

RECIPES FOR 13 UNUSUAL OR SPECIAL ROLLS

In times when bread was sold from door to door or on the market place by a huckster, the town baker included an extra loaf in each dozen to be sold, thereby making the number up to thirteen. The thirteenth loaf was kept by the huckster – doubtless after much haggling as to its price – in the form of a retainer, and since that time the Baker's Dozen has always numbered thirteen. The thirteen recipes given in this chapter are all for small rolls or buns, and they stem from different countries throughout the world.

MILK ROLLS

450g (1lb) flour
1 teaspoon salt
1 tablespoon sugar

⅛ litre (¼ pint) warm milk
25g (1oz) melted butter
15g (½oz) fresh yeast

Sift half the flour and the salt and sugar into a bowl. Heat the milk and butter till lukewarm and cream the yeast into them. Beat the liquid into the sifted flour and continue beating till the mixture forms bubbles. Stir in the remaining flour then knead the dough on a lightly floured board till the dough no longer sticks to the fingers. Gather into a ball and place in a greased bowl. Turn the dough ball in the bowl so that it is coated with grease on all sides. Prove till double in bulk, punch down and knead again lightly. Form the dough into 12 shapes, place on a greased baking sheet and prove again. Brush the rolls with beaten egg and bake at 200°C/400°F for about 15–20 minutes.

BLINIS (Russia)

A Russian bread made from buckwheat flour, blinis are traditionally eaten with sour cream and caviar. Buckwheat was used extensively in Russia from where it was introduced to other European countries. Its triangular grain has a black husk which caused the French to term it 'Blé noir'. Even today with the modern type of relentless mill, the black husk often adheres to the inner kernel after grinding and boulting, causing many to regard the black grains as being 'bad'.

Blinis are baked on an open griddle, rather in the manner of Scottish scones, and are eaten while still warm.

125g (4½oz) buckwheat
  flour
25g (1oz) fresh yeast
100ml (⅙ pint) warm milk
  and water
125g (4½oz) plain flour

½ teaspoon salt
1 tablespoon melted butter
1 egg
1 egg yolk
1 egg white

Place the buckwheat in a warm basin. Cream the yeast with the warm milk and water mixture and mix it with the buckwheat in the basin. Cover the basin with a damp cloth and prove till double in bulk. Sift the plain flour into another bowl and scatter the salt over the surface. Mix the butter, egg and egg yolk to a batter with the flour, adding a little warm milk if the mixture is too thick. Combine the two flour mixtures, adding more plain flour if the mixture is too sticky. Beat vigorously with a wooden spoon, cover and prove till double in bulk. Beat the egg white till stiff and fold into the blinis dough shortly before cooking. Have a greased griddle or heavy frying pan ready, and drop the blinis on to it in the manner of drop scones, The blinis should be the size of a small saucer. Spread with butter or sour cream while still hot and serve with caviar.

GRANNY HEWITT'S BROWNIES (Australia)

'I've got a loaf of bread and some murphies* that I
                                                      shook,†
Perhaps a loaf of brownie that I snaffled from the cook.
A nice leg of mutton, just a bit cut off the end,
Oh isn't it nice and cosy to be whaling in the Bend!'

* potatoes
† steal

Early Australian song, known variously as
The black fish song and *The whaler's rhyme*

This recipe is one which has been handed down in our family from one generation to the next. My people were originally all from the country and did their own baking as a matter of course. At shearing and mustering time brownies would be particularly in demand whenever the cry of 'Smoko' rose on the dusty air. Customarily made up in batches of eight to nine dozen, the brownies would be stored in a large tin tea chest, thence to be carried out to the stock-yards. Traditionally washed down with strong, black, sweet tea made in a billy, the brownies provided – and still provide – instant refreshment for the men and women of the land.

For 12 brownies

1½ *cups self-raising flour, or the equivalent of plain flour with 1 teaspoon baking powder*
¾ *cup sugar*
¼ *teaspoon salt*

1 *dessertspoon cinnamon*
1 *tablespoon butter*
1 *egg*
1 *teaspoon vanilla essence*
about ½ cup milk
handful of mixed dried fruit

Sift all the dry ingredients into a bowl. Rub in the butter with the fingertips, and then stir in the lightly beaten egg and the vanilla. Add just enough milk to make a soft but not sticky dough, and gently knead the fruit into the mixture. Note: as this dough is leavened through the baking powder and not yeast, kneading at this stage only continues till the fruit is smoothly incorporated in the dough. Press out the dough into a rectangle of 2½cm (1in) thickness, and stamp out square or round shapes. Transfer the brownies to a greased baking sheet, brush with milk, and strew with cinnamon and sugar. Bake at 200°C/400F for 10–15 minutes.

MARITOZZI ROMANI (Italy)

These Italian buns are a favourite breakfast bread in Rome. If your bread fever is not severe enough to get you out of bed early enough to prepare them for your own breakfast, try them in the afternoon to the accompaniment of creamy cappucino or espresso.

600g (1lb 5oz) flour
15g (½oz) fresh yeast
100g (4oz) sugar
¼ litre (½ pint) warm water
2 large eggs
4 tablespoons olive oil
125g (4½oz) raisins

Glaze
2½ tablespoons sugar
* blended with 2½*
* tablespoons water*

Sift the flour into a bowl and press a well into the centre. Crumble the yeast into the well and add one teaspoon of the sugar plus enough warm water to make a smooth paste with the yeast and sugar. Stir the yeast, sugar and water, drawing in a little of the flour from the sides of the well. Cover the bowl and prove till the yeast paste is bubbly. Beat the eggs and add them to the mixture together with the other ingredients. Working with the hand, make a cohesive dough of the ingredients, then turn out on to a floured board and knead for 5 minutes. Gather the dough into a ball, grease it and allow to prove till double in bulk. Punch down the dough, knead briefly then divide into pieces about the size of an egg. Place the Maritozzi on a greased baking sheet and prove again till puffy. Brush with glaze and bake at 200°C/400°F till golden – about 15 minutes.

PETITS PAINS AU CHOCOLAT (France)

A product of the French pâtisserie, petits pains au chocolat are a delight when served freshly baked at breakfast time. They are ideally suited to coffee or cocoa as they are filled with strips of chocolate.

500g (1lb 2oz) flour
100g (4oz) sugar
½ teaspoon salt
15g (½oz) fresh yeast
100ml (⅛ pint) warm water
100g (4oz) butter

1 egg
⅛ litre (¼ pint) warm milk
½ teaspoon vanilla essence
350g (12oz) cooking
  chocolate

Sift the flour, sugar and salt into a large bowl. Press a well into the centre. Dissolve the yeast in the warm water together with one teaspoon of sugar and pour it into the well. Stir the yeast and water in the well, drawing in a little flour to form a paste. Cover the bowl and prove till the yeast is bubbly. Melt and cool the butter and add it to the flour together with the beaten egg, milk and vanilla. Combine the ingredients with the hand, gather up and turn out on to a lightly floured board. Knead the dough for 10 minutes or until it is satiny and no longer sticks to the fingers. Return the dough to a greased bowl, cover and prove till double in bulk. Punch down and knead again lightly. Roll out to a thickness of 1cm (½in) and cut the dough into rounds with a glass or scone-cutter. Roll each round gently under a rolling pin to elongate it into an oval and make a slight trough down the centre of the oval with the fingertips. Place small pieces of broken chocolate down the length of the trough, fold the sides of the oval over the chocolate and pinch them together to seal. Turn the pinched edges under and place seam side down on greased baking sheets. Prove till puffy. Brush the petits pains with milk and bake them at 200°C/400°F till golden (about 15 minutes).

ČESKÉ KOLÁČE (Czechoslovakia)

Czechoslovakia is a country which enjoys a hearty, country type of cooking. Similar to Germany in its eating habits, the Czech loves his Houskové Knedlíky or bread dumplings (page 141) as much as he treasures his koláče and coffee served at the afternoon svačina. Famous not only for its beautiful capital Prague, the fairytale city, Czechoslovakia has also left the world a legacy of music by such composers as Dvořák and Janáček.

The koláče can be filled with almost any filling: marmalade, jam, cheesecake mixture, prunes or sweetened poppy-seeds. Recipes for both the cheese and prune fillings are given here, but with a little imagination, you can think of many more.

Dough
500g *(1 lb 2 oz) plain flour*
½ *teaspoon salt*
100g *(4 oz) sugar*
15g *(½ oz) fresh yeast*
¼ *litre (½ pint) warm milk*
   and water
100g *(4 oz) butter*
1 *egg yolk*
grated rind of one lemon

Cheesecake filling
2 *tablespoons soft butter*
75g *(2½ oz) sugar*
250g *(9 oz) ricotta or*
   cottage cheese
grated rind of one lemon
¼ *teaspoon vanilla essence*
2 *egg yolks*
75g *(2½ oz) sultanas*

Prune filling
250g (9oz) pitted prunes   *juice of one lemon*
60g (2oz) sugar   *grated rind of half a lemon*

Dough

Sift the flour, salt and sugar into a large bowl. Dissolve the yeast and a teaspoon of sugar in the warm milk and water and pour it into the centre of the flour. Stir with a little of the flour to make a paste and cover and allow to stand till the yeast paste is bubbly. Warm the butter till it is liquid and allow to cool to lukewarm. Add the butter, egg yolk and lemon rind to the flour and work the ingredients to a cohesive dough. Turn out on to a floured board and knead for five minutes. Gather the dough into a ball, grease it and return to the bowl to prove till double in bulk. Punch down and form into egg-sized balls. With both thumbs together press an indentation into each ball, place on a greased sheet and fill the well with the desired filling. Allow the koláče to prove till light and risen, brush with milk and bake at 200°C/400°F for 15–20 minutes. When cool dust with icing sugar.

Cheesecake filling

Cream the butter and sugar and add the egg yolks. Continue beating till the mixture is fluffy. Stir in the other ingredients.

Prune filling

Place the prunes in a saucepan and bring to the boil in enough water to cover. Add the sugar, lemon juice and rind and continue to simmer till the mixture is thick and the prunes are tender. Cool.

BAPS (Scotland)

This is a recipe for an early Scottish bun which is still baked in parts of Great Britain. It was taken for granted that the cook would put down a dough at about teatime in preparation for breakfast of the following day. This meant that somebody would have to get up in the middle of the night to punch down and re-knead the rising dough to prevent it spoiling. If you feel inclined to interrupt your sleep at midnight, well and good, but for those who prefer to sleep their eight hours at a stretch, here is an alternative for the bap-lover.

500g (1lb 2oz) flour
½ teaspoon salt
15g (½oz) fresh yeast for a
    slow, overnight proving
or
30g (1oz) fresh yeast for a
    quick rise

1 teaspoon sugar
¼ litre (½ pint) warm milk
    and water
60g (2oz) lard
milk for glazing

Sift the flour and salt into a bowl and press a well into the centre. Cream the yeast with the sugar and dissolve it in the milk and water. Pour the liquid into the well and stir to make a paste. Cover and prove briefly. Melt the lard and allow it to cool to blood heat. Pour over the flour and combine the ingredients thoroughly to form a slack dough. Add more milk if necessary. If using the smaller quantity of yeast allow to prove overnight, or, if the weather is warm, for a shorter period, till double in bulk. If using 30g (1oz) yeast the dough will be ready to shape into baps after an hour or two. Punch down the dough and form into eight pieces about the size of a goose egg. Flatten each ball into an oval, place on a well-floured tin, cover and prove for 15 minutes. Brush with milk and bake at 200°C/400°F till firm.

DANISH PASTRIES

Although these pastries originate from Denmark they have become a familiar sight in bakers' windows throughout the world. Their fanciful shapes and flaky texture make them deservedly popular.

350g (12oz) flour
¼ teaspoon salt
30g (1oz) fresh yeast
60g (2oz) castor sugar
150ml (¼ pint) warm milk
250g (9oz) butter
1 egg
beaten egg for glaze
vanilla icing

Almond filling
60g (2oz) ground sweet almonds
50g (2oz) castor sugar
a little beaten egg

Apple filling
3 cooking apples
1 teaspoon butter
grated rind and juice of one lemon
3 tablespoons sugar

Dough

Sift the flour and salt into a large bowl. Cream the yeast and sugar and stir into the warm milk. Heat a quarter of the butter and allow it to cool to lukewarm. Mix it with the yeast and milk and then add to the flour in the bowl. Crack the egg into the yeast and milk liquid, and mix with the flour to form a smooth dough. Cover the bowl and prove till double in bulk. Punch down the dough, turn out on to a floured board and knead lightly. Roll out into a long rectangle 1cm (½in) thick and indent the upper two-thirds of the dough working from the short edge with the fingertips. Cut the remaining butter into small pieces and press lightly into the indentations. Fold butter-free third over the middle third and then the upper third over it to make an envelope. Press the edges of the dough together to seal. Roll out the rectangle to its original size and fold again. Place in the refrigerator to cool for 15 minutes. Roll out and fold again twice in the same manner, and return to the refrigerator for 15 minutes. Roll out the dough to a thickness of 1cm (½in) and divide into 12 pieces. Shape into one of the traditional Danish pastry shapes of cartwheel, comb, envelope or pinwheel and fill with a little filling or jam. Place on greased baking sheets, cover and prove till double in bulk. Brush with beaten egg and bake at 200°C/400°F for 20–25 minutes. While still warm brush with vanilla icing.

Almond filling
Mix the ground almonds and sugar with enough beaten egg to bind.

Apple filling
Peel and core the apples. Rub out a saucepan with the butter and slice the apples into it. Add the lemon juice and rind, cover, and cook very gently till the apples are tender. Purée the apples, add the sugar and one tablespoon water and cook gently stirring all the while till they form a paste. Cool to lukewarm before using in the pastries.

DEBRECZINER BRETZELN (Hungary)

The Bretzel, with its characteristic shape, has become a familiar sight in restaurants and beer halls of Europe as well as in the rest of the Western world. In Hungary the Bretzeln can often be seen at fairs skewered on long poles, their shining loops being offered to the passersby or to guests seated in beer gardens.

500g (1lb 2oz) flour
a little salt
15g (½oz) fresh yeast
scant ¼ litre (½ pint)
  lukewarm milk

125g (4½oz) melted pork
  lard
3 tablespoons sour cream
lukewarm water if necessary
milk for glazing

Sift the flour and salt into a bowl. Dissolve the yeast in the lukewarm milk and add the lard and sour cream. Combine the liquid with the flour and mix well. Knead till smooth, adding a little lukewarm water if the dough is too stiff or crumbly. Prove till doubled in bulk and then form about 40 Bretzeln from the dough by rolling it into strips the thickness of a pencil and bending into a Bretzel shape: take the two ends of the dough and bend them back towards each other so that they cross over. Place the Bretzeln on greased baking sheets and bake at 190°C/400°F till golden (about 40 minutes). While still warm, brush with a little milk.

POPOVERS (America)

Popovers are frequently served in America at breakfast and are ideally suited to that meal as the popover has roomy cavities inside its seemingly sound walls which make delicious pouches for honey, jam and butter. They are best baked in cast iron popover forms as they reach the high temperature needed to make these little buns 'pop over' and more than double their uncooked height.

150g (5oz) flour	3 eggs
½ teaspoon salt	¼ litre (½ pint) milk

Sift the flour and salt twice. Beat the eggs lightly and combine with the milk. Mix the flour and milk to make a batter which has the consistency of double cream. Heat the popover baking forms till they are sizzling, brush with melted butter and fill each cup half full. Bake at 220°C/425°F for 15 minutes and then lower the temperature to 190°C/375°F and bake a further 20–30 minutes.

PITTA OR PITA (Middle East)

Although Pita is a Greek word representing our equivalent
'pie', this Middle Eastern bread is found not only in Greece
but in such countries as the Lebanon, Armenia and Cyprus.
It is regarded as being a 'flat bread' even though it is leavened,
and is unusual in that it forms a hollow in the middle during
baking. Pita are invariably filled and halved in the Lebanese
manner, or served with the filling on top – like a pizza to
which it is closely related.

2 tablespoons honey   15g (½oz) fresh yeast
1 tablespoon salt   800g (1lb 12oz) flour
½ litre (¾ pint) hot water

Stir the honey and salt into the hot water and continue stirring till dissolved. Allow the water to cool to lukewarm and
add the yeast. Stir till the yeast dissolves. Sift the flour into
a bowl and pour the yeast liquid over it. Combine the ingredients thoroughly till smooth. The dough should be fairly
stiff; if necessary, adjust the amount of flour or water at this
stage. Turn out on to a lightly floured board and knead for
5 minutes. Gather the dough into a ball and oil it. Return to
the bowl, cover and prove till double in bulk. Punch down
and knead lightly. Divide the dough into twelve pieces roughly the same size and shape each into a smooth, seamless ball.
Space the pita balls on a floured surface, cover, and allow to
rest for 10 minutes. Meanwhile, heat the oven to 230°C/
450°F. Flatten each ball into a round about 20–25cm (8–10
in) in diameter, being careful not to pucker the dough in the
process as this would prevent it from becoming hollow in the
middle during baking. Lift the pita on to a greased oven
sheet and prepare the next. Bake two or three at a time as
low in the oven as possible. Do not flatten the other balls
until there is room in the oven for them to be baked, as they
will rise prematurely and be difficult to handle. Bake till the

bases are browned – if the top of the pita is pale, it can be browned briefly under the grill. Serve hot, either slit open and filled, or as an accompaniment to a hot dish.

CROISSANT (France)

The famous croissant, which makes France unforgettable for every tourist, has a long history which dates back to 1686 when the city of Budapest was laid siege to by the Turks. The Turks had burrowed underground passages to catch the people of Budapest unawares, and it was the town's bakers – already hard at work in the early hours of the morning – who heard the enemy's scufflings underfoot and apprised the city fathers of the danger. The assailants were put to flight and the bakers were put to work designing a new pastry to commemorate the victory. Thus was born the croissant, its crescent shape moulded after the emblem of the Turkish flag.

The art of croissant-making is similar to that of making puff pastry and requires a little practice, but if you have ever breakfasted in Paris or Bamberg on croissants or Butterhörnchen, the memory will keep you persevering till you are satisfied.

500g (1lb 2oz) flour
20g (⅔oz) fresh yeast
2 teaspoons sugar

scant ¼ litre (½ pint) warm milk
½ teaspoon salt
200g (7oz) butter

Sift the flour into a bowl and press a well into the centre. Cream the yeast and sugar with a fork and add a little of the warm milk. Place the yeast and milk in the well and stir to form a paste with some of the flour. Cover and allow the yeast to 'sponge' till bubbly. Add the salt to the flour and combine the ingredients in the bowl with the hand till they are cohesive. Gradually add the rest of the milk and beat with a wooden spoon till smooth and the dough leaves the sides of the bowl. Cover and allow to prove briefly for about 20 minutes in a warm place. Meanwhile, prepare the butter. The butter should be firm but not hard. Roll it out into a rectangle between sheets of waxed paper and put aside. Roll out the dough to a thickness of about 1½cm (½in) and the shape of a long rectangle. Place the butter slab on the dough and fold the left and then the right flaps over the butter, making sure that the edges come together neatly. Roll out the envelope in one direction and fold in three in the same manner again. Chill the dough for some hours. When ready to use, roll out and fold the dough three times again and chill for one hour. Roll out to a thickness of ½cm (¼in) and cut the dough into squares measuring 20×20cm (8×8in). Divide each square diagonally. Starting at the long base of the triangle, roll up each piece of dough and bend into a crescent. Place the croissants on a floured baking sheet, cover and prove till double in bulk. Brush with beaten egg and bake in an oven pre-heated to 200°C/400°F for the first 5 minutes, then lower the temperature to 180°C/350°F and bake a further 15–20 minutes.

CRAILSHEIMER HORAFFEN (Germany)

Not only these historic rolls, but also the residents of Crailsheim bear the nickname 'Horaffen', meaning 'hairy apes', in memory of their imaginative townswoman who bore the office of lady mayoress in the year 1379. At that time Crailsheim was under siege by enemy forces who proved to be no match for the mayoress who brought about their downfall – and speedy withdrawal – by the simple expedient of exposing her bared buttocks, upon which a horrible face was painted, at a handy hole in the town wall overlooking the enemy camp. So much for fourteenth century superstition and so-called female 'vanity'!

30g (1oz) fresh yeast
¼ litre (½ pint) lukewarm
   milk
1 teaspoon sugar
150g (5½oz) butter
150g (5½oz) sugar

2 eggs
500g (1lb 2oz) flour
1 teaspoon salt
grated rind 1 lemon
1 egg for glaze
vanilla icing

Crumble the yeast, add a little of the warm milk and 1 tea-spoon sugar. Stir until the yeast dissolves, cover and stand in a warm place till air bubbles appear on the surface of the mixture. Cream together the butter and sugar, then beat in the 2 eggs alternately with the yeast mixture. Add the remaining milk, the flour sifted with 1 teaspoon salt, and the grated rind of the lemon. Beat the mixture vigorously with a wooden spoon till bubbles appear on the surface of the dough and it is quite smooth. Cover and allow to prove for half an hour, punch down and form the mass into rolls of thumb thickness. Cut these rolls into 10cm (4in) sections and shape each into a half-circle. Join two half-circles together in such a way as to form a figure '3' lying on its side (this depicts the mayoral buttocks). Continue to form the Horaffen till all the sections are paired; place on greased baking sheets, cover and allow to prove till puffed. Beat an egg and brush it sparingly on the pastries, then bake at 200°C/400°F for 15–25 minutes. After the Horaffen have cooled, brush with a little vanilla icing.

Chapter Four

'THE STAFF OF LIFE'

RECIPES FOR EVERDAY SALT BREADS

FRENCH BREAD

THIS FAMOUS BREAD IS KNOWN THROUGHOUT the world and is as French as the Eiffel Tower and Château Neuf du Pape. The sticks or *baguettes* of bread are a familiar sight in France, tucked under the arm of a homeward-bound cyclist or packed into tall baskets at a boulangerie. The housewife is particular about the quality of the bread she brings to her table and is even known to specify which part of the oven she wants her bread to be baked in so that the crust will be just to her liking. If you have eaten French bread in France, expect your own French bread to taste a little different, as flour varies in taste and texture from country to country.

20g (⅔oz) fresh yeast	1 tablespoon salt
2 teaspoons sugar	1 tablespoon lemon juice
½ litre (¾ pint) milk or	1–2 tablespoons butter
water at blood heat	850g (1lb 14oz) flour

In a large bowl dissolve the yeast and sugar in the warm milk or water. Add salt, lemon juice and butter and enough flour to make a soft dough. Turn out on to a floured board and knead for about 10 minutes until elastic. Grease the dough lightly and return to the bowl. Prove till doubled in bulk. Punch down and divide into three parts. Roll out each to a long rectangle. Starting at the long edge, roll up tightly and transfer to a greased baking sheet. Repeat with the other pieces of dough making sure that the loaves are placed seam side down on the sheets. With a sharp knife slash the baguettes diagonally along their length. Cover and prove till light and risen. Brush with water and bake at 200°C/400°F brushing once or twice more during the baking process. They should be ready to take out of the oven after 45–50 minutes.

ZWIEBELBROT
German Onion Bread

½ litre (¾ pint) warm milk
¼ litre (scant ½ pint) warm
   water
4 teaspoons salt
2 tablespoons oil
2 tablespoons sugar

800g (1lb 12oz) plain flour
30g (1oz) fresh yeast
3 tablespoons caraway seeds
250g (9oz) chopped onion
250g (9oz) rye flour
2 tablespoons cream

Scald the milk and water and add the salt, oil and sugar. Set aside to cool to blood heat. Sift the plain flour and beat into the milk and yeast. Add the caraway seeds and chopped onion. Start to knead in the rye flour with the hand, and, when stiff enough, gather into a ball and turn out on to a floured board. Knead in the remaining rye flour or enough to make a stiffish dough. Continue kneading for 10 minutes, form the dough into a ball and place in a greased bowl. Turn the dough in the bowl to ensure that it is greased on all sides, cover and prove till double in bulk. Punch down and knead lightly. Divide into two large or three smaller loaves, and place in greased loaf pans. Prove again till well risen, brush with cream and sprinkle with salt. Bake at 200°C/400°F for about 1 hour.

VIENNESE MILK BREAD

This is a light milk loaf which has a fine texture and toasts very well. The dough can be braided and baked free, or shaped into a long loaf surmounted by a two-stranded rope.

1kg (2¼lb) flour
½ litre (¾ pint) milk
60g (2oz) butter
1 teaspoon salt

1 egg
30g (1oz) fresh yeast
1 teaspoon sugar

Sift the flour into a bowl and press a well into its centre. Scald the milk and let the butter melt in it and cool to luke-warm. Sprinkle the salt over the flour and crack the egg into the well in the flour. Cream the yeast and sugar and add to the lukewarm milk. Stir to dissolve. Pour the milk into the well in the flour and mix with the egg to form a paste. Work-ing with the hands combine all the ingredients in the bowl to make a soft dough. Turn out on to a floured board and knead till smooth and elastic. Return to the clean, greased bowl, cover and prove till doubled in bulk. Punch down the dough, knead lightly and form into two balls. Pinch off a little dough from each ball and reserve. Shape into two fat sausage-shaped loaves and place on greased baking sheets. From the reserved dough fashion two ropes made of two strands of dough twisted together, and place these along the length of each loaf. Allow to prove till well risen; brush with a little milk and bake at 200°C/400°F till golden – about 50 minutes.

WHOLEWHEAT BREAD

This bread has a heavier texture than ordinary wheaten bread due to the use of wholewheat flour or meal and the addition of a little rye flour. It makes a moist loaf which keeps well.

300g (11oz) strong plain
  flour
400g (14oz) wholewheat
  flour
100g (4oz) rye flour
30g (1oz) fresh yeast

1 tablespoon sugar
lukewarm water
½ litre (¾ pint) milk
2 tablespoons butter
2 teaspoons salt

Sift the strong plain flour into a large bowl. Add the whole-wheat and rye flour and stir with the hand to mix roughly. Cream the yeast and sugar and dissolve in a little lukewarm water. Bring the milk to the boil, remove from the heat and stir in the butter. Let the butter melt and when the milk has cooled to blood heat, stir in the creamed yeast. Add the salt to the liquid and pour it into the centre of the flours. Combine all the ingredients well, adjusting the texture of the dough to make it kneadable either by the addition of a little more milk or plain flour. Gather into a ball and turn out on to a floured board. Knead for 8–10 minutes. Roll into a ball and place in a greased bowl, turning the ball so that it is greased on all sides. Prove till double in bulk. Punch down and knead lightly. Form into three loaves or divide the dough between three bread pans, cover and prove till risen. Bake at 220°C/425°F for 10 minutes, then lower the temperature to 200°C/400°F and bake a further 30–40 minutes.

TOM'S BELLY

Tom serves his 'Belly' on cold winter nights to admiring and famished dinner guests, and invariably plies them with steaming sauerkraut and Bratäpfel as well.

1½kg (3½lb) lean belly of
  pork
1 clove garlic
1 large onion
2 tablespoons chopped parsley

2 slices rye bread
500g (1lb 2oz) pork and
  veal mince
150g (5oz) mushrooms
1 finely sliced carrot

pimento or ground cloves
fresh marjoram
salt and pepper

750g (1¾lb) mixed wheat
and rye dough (see next
recipe) which has proved
once
caraway seeds

Cut a pocket in the pork belly and rub with the cut garlic clove. Chop the onion finely and fry gently together with the parsley. Cube the rye bread and add to the onion. Fry the mixture till the bread croûtons are golden. Mix in the pork and veal mince, mushrooms, carrot, and seasonings and loosely stuff the belly with the mixture. Sew the opening up, and if any of the filling oozes out, place the belly in an oven bag. Place the belly fatty side down in the oven and bake at 240°C/475°F for 10 minutes, then reduce the temperature to 180°C/350°F and bake a further 2–3 hours. Test to see if the belly is adequately cooked by pushing a skewer into its centre – if the skewer enters the belly easily it is adequately cooked. Transfer to a rack and allow to cool to lukewarm. Wrap the prepared dough round the cooked belly, sealing the seams by pinching firmly together. Place seam side down in a clean baking dish. Brush with a little beaten egg, sprinkle with caraway seeds and bake at 200°C/400°F till golden.

SIMPLE RYE BREAD

This is a basic dark bread which is very easy to make, keeps well and makes excellent sandwiches. It is shaped into loaves by hand and baked 'free'.

1kg (2¼lb) plain flour
1kg (2¼lb) rye flour
800ml (1¾ pints) lukewarm
water

30g (1oz) fresh yeast
1½ tablespoons of salt
1 tablespoon caraway seeds

Sift the flours into a large bowl, and warm the flour in the oven till it has the same temperature as your hand. Pour a quarter of the water into the middle of the flour and crumble the yeast into it. Stir the yeast till it dissolves, drawing in a little of the flour from the sides of the well which the water has made. Dust the yeast paste with a little flour, cover the bowl and prove for 10–15 minutes. Now add the rest of the water, the salt and the caraway seeds and working with the hand combine the ingredients thoroughly. Gather the dough into a ball and turn it out on to a lightly floured board. Knead firmly for 10 minutes, return the dough to the bowl, cover and prove till double in bulk. Knead the dough once again for about 5 minutes, and divide it into two equal parts. Shape each part into a long sausage shape about 12½cm (5in) in diameter. Roll each loaf in a floured tea towel so that it will maintain its shape, and prove till double in bulk. Bake in the middle of the oven for 10 minutes at 240°C/475°F then reduce the temperature to 200°C/400°F and bake a further 40–50 minutes. Five minutes before the loaves are done, brush with milk to glaze or, after baking dust them with a little rye flour.

BAGELS – basic (Eastern Europe)

Bagels originated in Eastern Europe. The Russians called them *Bubliki* and many songs were written about them. At fairs in Russian towns bagels could be seen for sale, threaded like quoits on a string. Being circular, the rings were credited with all sorts of magic properties 'having no beginning and no end', and were said to bring good luck.

Bagels and hard-boiled eggs were part of a traditional Jewish wake, symbolizing by their roundness the cycle of life without end.

To make 12 bagels

350g (12oz) flour	1 egg
1½ teaspoons salt	4 litres (7 pints) boiling
2 tablespoons castor sugar	water
10g (⅓oz) fresh yeast	1 egg yolk mixed with 1
125ml (scant ¼ pint)	tablespoon water
lukewarm water	caraway seeds, poppyseeds,
oil	or salt crystals

Sift flour, salt and two tablespoons sugar into a large mixing bowl. Dissolve yeast in half the lukewarm water, stir well. Add oil and the rest of the lukewarm water to the yeast. Beat the egg and add to the yeast mixture. Make a well in the centre of the flour. Pour the yeast and egg mixture into the well, mix, and knead to a smooth dough. This should take three to four minutes. Cover the bowl with a cloth and allow the dough to prove till double in size. Turn out on to a lightly floured board and knead till elastic. Divide into 12 equal portions and shape each portion into a roll about 10 cm (4in) long, joining the ends to make a ring. Allow the bagels to rest for 15 minutes or until they start to rise. Using a large saucepan, bring the water to the boil, then dissolve 3 tablespoons of sugar in it. Drop the bagels into the water one at a time so that the water does not come off the boil. Allow to simmer gently for 10–15 minutes till they rise to the surface. Lift the bagels out of the water and drain. Place on lightly oiled baking sheets and brush with the beaten egg yolk and water. Sprinkle with caraway seeds, poppyseeds or salt crystals and bake at 200°C/400°F for 25–30 minutes.

BAGELS – rye

15g (½oz) fresh yeast	1 teaspoon salt
30g (1oz) castor sugar	1 egg yolk
60g (2oz) butter	500g (1lb 2oz) rye flour
¼ litre (½ pint) milk or	mixed with wholewheat,
water	soya flour

Cream the yeast with a teaspoon of the sugar. Put the butter, milk, remaining sugar and salt into a saucepan and place over a very gentle heat until the butter is melted. Leave to cool to lukewarm then mix with the dissolved yeast. Add this, together with the beaten egg yolk, to the flour and knead to a firm dough. Cover with a cloth and leave to prove till dough begins to rise; about one hour. Then knead again and roll into small pieces of finger thickness and about 10cm (4in) in length. Fashion each roll into a ring by pinching the ends together, then allow the bagels to rise for 10 minutes. Drop the bagels into simmering water one at a time, and allow to cook gently till they swim to the surface. Remove with a slotted spoon and drain thoroughly. Place the bagels on greased baking sheets and bake at 200°C/400°F for 20–30 minutes till crisp and golden.

Bagels – onion
To the basic bagel recipe (p. 87) add ½ cup dried onions, and sprinkle the bagels with additional dried onion just before baking.

Bagels – raisin and almond
To the basic bagel recipe (p. 87) add 1 cup of plumped raisins and ½ cup chopped almonds mixed with a teaspoon of grated lemon rind.

TORTILLAS (Mexico)

As Mexican as sarsaparilla and sombreroes, the tortilla, together with a large variety of beans, forms the staple of the Mexican diet. Although leavened breads are known in Mexico they have never been as popular there as in Western countries.

Just as fresh pasta tastes so much better than the bought, so too do homemade tortillas. The following recipe for tortillas is followed by one for *panuchos* or stuffed tortillas.

THE STAFF OF LIFE

Tortillas
250g (9oz) maize flour   *175 ml (scant ⅓ pint)*
  (e.g. Quaker's Masa   *warm water*
  Harina)   *½ teaspoon salt*

In a bowl combine the ingredients and work to a smooth soft dough. Have 10cm (4in) squares of greaseproof paper ready so that the tortillas can be flattened between them without sticking. Divide the dough into twenty equal pieces and shape each into a ball. Flatten the dough between two layers of greaseproof paper to a width of 10cm (4in). If the dough sticks to the paper it is too moist, in which case add more maize flour. The tortillas are fried in hot oil.

Panuchos
  Black bean paste   *Filling*
  250g (9oz) black turtle   *1 onion*
    beans   *⅛ litre (¼ pint) vinegar*
  ½ teaspoon chilli powder   *2 cooked chicken breasts*
  1 tablespoon salt   *1 small head lettuce*
     4 tomatoes

Wash and sort the beans. Put them in a saucepan together with the chilli and cover with water. Bring the water to the boil and simmer for about three hours, adding more water as necessary to keep the beans covered. When tender, add the salt and allow nearly all the liquid to boil away. Purée the beans in a blender and keep warm.

To make the panuchos, chop the onion and soak it in cold water to cover for 5 minutes. Drain the onion and bring it to the boil in the vinegar. Take the saucepan off the heat and let the onion cool in the vinegar. Drain the onion and reserve it. Chop the chicken finely and shred the head of lettuce. Slice the tomatoes finely. Prepare about twenty tortillas and fry them a few at a time in hot oil, turning them frequently until they are golden. Slit the tortillas where they are puffed at the edge, being careful not to tear them.

Fill the pocket with a little of the black bean paste and fry the tortilla in a little hot oil filled side up till browned. Drain the tortillas and top each with a slice of tomato and a little of the lettuce, chicken and onion.

NAN (India)

Nan is one of the few Asian breads, and probably came to India, its home, by way of the Middle Eastern sea traders, as it is closely related to the Morrocan and Armenian forms of pita. It is baked in a very hot oven and eaten straight away – usually to the accompaniment of such a tantalizing dish as Kofta. Following the recipe for Nan is one for Pooris, which is also an Indian bread, but in this case it is deep-fried and the dough flavoured with celery seed.

500–550g (1lb 2oz–1lb 4oz) flour
15g (½oz) fresh yeast
¼ litre (½ pint) lukewarm water
1 tablespoon honey

2 tablespoons buttermilk
2 tablespoons oil
1 egg
2 teaspoons salt
melted butter
poppyseeds (optional)

Sift 500g (1lb 2oz) flour into a bowl and press a well into the centre. Dissolve the yeast in a little of the lukewarm water and mix with the honey, buttermilk and remaining water. Add the oil, egg and salt and stir till dissolved. Using a wooden spoon, combine the liquid with the flour – the dough will be very sticky at this stage. Add only enough of the remaining flour to stop the spoon from dragging in the flour. Leave the dough in the bowl and, with your floured hand, work for a while till the dough is just manageable. Leave in the bowl, cover and prove till well risen. Flour one hand and punch down the dough, pressing out any air bubbles. Transfer the dough to a floured board and shape into 12 balls. Cover the balls and let rest for about ten minutes. Heat the oven to

230°C/450°F. Flatten two of the balls and transfer to greased baking sheets. Brush with melted butter and sprinkle sparingly with poppyseeds. Bake at the bottom of the oven for about 7 minutes, then brown briefly under the grill. Serve at once.

POORIS (India)

100g (4oz) semolina
100g (4oz) plain flour
100g (4oz) wholemeal flour
½ teaspoon salt
½ teaspoon celery seed

1 tablespoon soft butter
1 tablespoon yoghurt
⅛ litre (¼ pint) water
vegetable oil

Place the semolina in a bowl and sift the other flours over it. Add the salt and celery seed and rub in the softened butter till the flour resembles coarse meal. Mix in the yoghurt and enough water to make a firm dough. Knead for 10 minutes and roll into a ball. Grease the dough ball with a little oil, wrap in plastic and cool in the refrigerator for at least 1 hour. Shape the dough into 20 balls and return them to the plastic wrapper. Heat oil for deep frying. Take one ball at a time and flatten into a 10cm (4in) round. Drop into the oil and hold under the surface so that all sides are cooking at once. When the poori becomes puffed, turn it over and fry a further half minute. Drain on paper towels and keep warm. Repeat with the remaining dough.

ZWIEBACK

'Zwieback' means literally 'twice baked'. It is made by toasting bread in a slow oven till it is very dry and light and delicately coloured. The zwieback can be coated with various pastes prior to being baked, nuts and malt being the favourite coating. If there is a baby in the family, or illness, zwieback are ideal as a means of light nutrition.

500g (1lb 2oz) flour
35g (1⅙oz) fresh yeast
6og (2oz) sugar

½ litre (¾ pint) warm milk
pinch salt
grated rind of half a lemon

Place the flour in a bowl and press a well into the centre. Crumble the yeast into the well and mix to a paste with a little of the sugar and warm milk. Cover and stand in a warm place till the mixture 'sponges'. Mix in the salt and lemon rind and beat with a wooden spoon till the dough leaves the sides of the bowl. Prove for about 30–40 minutes and then shape the dough into rolls with a diameter of 6cm (2½in). Place the rolls lengthwise on greased baking sheets, cover and prove a further 20–30 minutes. Bake at 190–200°C/ 375–400°F for 30 minutes. On the following day cut the rolls into slices 1cm (½in) thick and bake again till golden. Turn the slices and bake till the reverse side is the same colour.

MAKRONENZWIEBACK

Zwieback slices
6og (2oz) marzipan
6og (2oz) icing sugar

1 egg white
a little rum

Prepare a paste from the last four ingredients. Spread over the zwieback slices and bake at 190°C/375°F for 30 minutes or until golden.

BOSTON STEAMED BROWN BREAD
(America)

This bread dates back to the times of the early American settlers who were learning to make use of cornmeal in baking their bread. The resultant loaf is dark in colour with a distinctive perfume of molasses.

200g (7oz) yellow
  cornmeal
200g (7oz) rye flour
200g (7oz) wholemeal flour
1 teaspoon salt

1 teaspoon baking soda
scant ½ litre (¾ pint)
  buttermilk
150ml (¼ pint) molasses
100g (4oz) raisins

Combine the dry ingredients thoroughly and then stir in buttermilk, molasses and raisins. Spoon into greased cylindrical pipe forms to two-thirds the height. Cover the tops with buttered foil and tie so as to make an airtight seal. Place on an iron trivet in a large saucepan and fill the saucepan with boiling water which comes half way up the outside of the tin. Cover the saucepan and steam the bread for 1½–2 hours, adding more water to the saucepan when necessary.

NORTHERN ENGLAND OATMEAL AND RYE BREAD

This is an English country bread which combines wholemeal flour with rolled oats and rye. The loaf is moist and fragrant and keeps well.

500g (1lb 2oz) plain flour
500g (1lb 2oz) wholemeal
  flour
250g (9oz) rye flour
scant 120g (9oz) rolled oats
2 teaspoons salt
30g (1oz) fresh yeast

a little sugar
¼ litre (½ pint) warm milk
  and water
1 tablespoon molasses
100ml (⅛ pint) oil
cream or top of the milk for
  glazing

Place all the flour and oats in a large bowl and allow to stand at room temperature for a while. Press a well into the centre of the flour and scatter the salt over the outer edges of the flour. Cream the yeast with a little sugar and dissolve it in two tablespoons of the warm milk and water. Pour into the well in the flour, and mix to form a paste. Cover the bowl and allow to stand till the yeast mixture is bubbly. Heat the rest of the milk and water and add the molasses and oil to it. Stir to mix the ingredients and let cool till they are lukewarm. Pour the milk and molasses into the flour, and mix all the ingredients to a smooth dough, adding a little more plain wheaten flour or liquid to make a dough which is not too soft or sticky. Turn out on to a floured board and knead for 10–15 minutes. The dough will have a harsh feeling under the hands but should be elastic at the end of the kneading time. Gather the dough into a ball and grease lightly on all sides. Cover and prove till doubled in bulk. Divide into two or three portions and knead each lightly. Shape into loaves and decorate by slashing with a sharp knife or pressing the finger-tips into the loaf to make a pattern. Prove once again, brush with cream and bake in a hot (220°C/425°F) oven for 10 minutes, then reduce the heat to 200°C/400°F and bake a further hour, basting the loaves once or twice during the baking period with cream.

GRISSINI (Italian Breadsticks)

The Grissino or breadstick came originally from the northern Italian city of Torino and has since become a familiar sight on tables throughout the world.

340g (12oz) flour
½ teaspoon salt
20g (⅔oz) fresh yeast
2 tablespoons warm milk
2 tablespoons olive oil

⅛ litre (¼ pint) or less warm water
1 egg white for glaze
coarse salt

Sift the flour and salt into a bowl and press a well into the centre of the flour. Dissolve the yeast in the warm milk and oil and pour into the well in the flour. Stir to make a paste and then cover the bowl and let it stand in a warm place till the yeast paste is bubbly. Add enough warm water to make a stiffish dough, turn out on to a floured board and knead till elastic. Gather the dough into a ball and grease lightly with a little olive oil. Return to the bowl, cover and allow to prove till double in bulk. Punch down the dough and lay on a floured board. Fold it over on itself several times till quite smooth and then shape into a roll. Cut into 30 slices and shape each slice into a slim pencil of dough. Place on a greased baking sheet, leaving at least 3cm (1¼in) between each grissino to allow for expansion. Prove till light and puffed, brush with the egg white and sprinkle with salt. Bake at 230°C/450°F for 5 minutes, then lower the temperature to 200°C/400°F and bake till done. The grissini should be quite dry inside when finished. Store in airtight jars when cool.

GRISSINI AL FORMAGGIO

Use the above recipe and add two tablespoons of finely grated hard cheese, such as parmesan, after sifting the flour.

SCHWÄBISCHES BAUERNBROT, FRANKENLAIB, OBERBAYRISCHES BAUERNBROT AND SIEBENBÜRGENER GRIEBENBROT
(Germany)

The following four recipes are for *Bauernbrot*, or peasant bread, which is eaten in its native country, Germany, by town and country dwellers alike. The bread is hearty and rugged with a personality all its own, and varies greatly from one region to another. Germany alone boasts some two hundred varieties of bread, from the breakfast *Semmel*, or roll, to the fruited Christmas *Dresdner Christstollen*, and with the present interest in many-grained loaves, the variety promises to increase rather than decline. For several years I lived in a quiet corner of Franconia and shared adjoining gardens with the local baker. *Bäcker* Burger would rise every morning at a quarter to four to fire his vast ovens and put down the first doughs of the day – these would be baked into hundreds of rolls which would then be delivered from door to door by the *Bäckerjunge* in time to be served still warm at breakfast, alongside pots of sweet butter, berry jams and steaming black coffee. Herr Burger's one lament was for the shortage of apprentices to ensure the continuation of his trade, for this, combined with changing industrial patterns poses the largest threat to the family bakery.

Here then, is as tempting a quartet of sour-dough country breads as can be found – Frankenlaib, Siebenbürgener Griebenbrot, and the Bauernbrot of Schwaben and Oberbayern.

To make the sour-dough

Mix enough rye or wholemeal rye flour with ⅛ litre (¼ pint) of lukewarm water to make a porridge-like paste. Spoon the sour 'starter' into a jar with a screw-top lid and close securely – the lid must have an airtight fit. After one day unscrew the lid and add a little milk or sour milk. Replace the lid on the jar and leave for another two to three days. Stir occasionally during this period and do not allow the starter to become chilled: it should be kept at room temperature. The sour-dough will be ready when it gives off a good sour odour. Now add a further ⅛ litre (¼ pint) of lukewarm water and enough rye or wholemeal rye flour to make a porridge-like paste and reseal the jar. Leave to stand overnight and by the morning the sour-dough will be ready to use.

SCHWÄBISCHES BAUERNBROT

The housewives of Schwaben are purported to be Germany's cleanest and most efficient. The countryside is friendly, the houses shine, and inside there is bound to be some sour-dough ripening on the tiled stove, amongst the perfume of apples and floor polish.

250g (9oz) sour-dough
½ litre (¾ pint) lukewarm
water
20g (⅔oz) fresh yeast
500g (1lb 2oz) strong plain
flour

500g (1lb 2oz) plain flour
5 teaspoons salt
4 medium-sized boiled
potatoes

Mix the sour-dough with half the lukewarm water. Crumble the yeast into it and stir till dissolved. Add a quarter of the flour and stir till the mixture is smooth. Put the rest of the flour into a large bowl and press a well into the centre. Spoon the yeast sponge into the well, cover the bowl with a cloth and stand the bowl in a warm place, or at least where there are no draughts, till the following morning. On the following morning, add the remaining warm water, salt and grated potatoes. Knead for ten minutes on a floured board, dust the dough with a little flour, cover and prove for about one hour or until well risen. Form two round loaves and cut the dough in four places with a sharp knife. Transfer the loaves to greased baking sheets and prove briefly once again. Brush with a little lukewarm water and bake at 230°C/450°F on the lowest rack in the oven for 60–75 minutes. Dust with a little white flour when baked.

FRANKENLAIB

Laib can mean either 'loaf' or 'body' and these big, heavy loaves are well-described by either term. They are set to prove in round rush baskets, from which they derive their characteristic rippled surface. Try serving the bread with beer and smoked ham with perhaps the addition of a good camembert.

300g (11oz) sour-dough
½ litre (¾ pint) lukewarm
   water
1kg (2¼lb) rye flour
5 teaspoons salt

1 tablespoon fennel powder
1 tablespoon aniseed
a few poppyseeds
   (optional)

The day before the bread is to be baked, mix the sour-dough with half the lukewarm water and stir till the paste is quite smooth. Cover with a cloth and stand in a warm place to prove overnight. On the following morning add the remaining lukewarm water and other ingredients to the sour-dough and mix thoroughly. Turn out on to a floured board and knead vigorously till the dough is smooth – about 10 minutes. Roll the dough into a ball, cover and prove for about 1½ hours. Shape the dough into a large loaf or two smaller ones and prove again, this time in a basket which has been rubbed with flour on the inside. Cover the basket with a cloth and prove till the dough is well risen. Turn out on to a greased and floured baking sheet, dust with a little rye flour or poppyseeds and bake at 240°C/475°F for the first 15 minutes, then reduce the temperature to 200°C/400°F and bake another 70–80 minutes.

OBERBAYRISCHES BAUERNBROT

250g (9oz) sour-dough
approx. ¾ litre (1¼ pints)
   lukewarm water
600g (1lb 6oz) wholemeal rye
   flour or plain rye flour
   (can be mixed half and
   half)

300g (11oz) wheaten flour
5 teaspoons salt
1½ tablespoons caraway seeds
1½ tablespoons fennel
   powder
1 tablespoon coriander
rolled oats

On the evening before the bread is to be baked, mix the prepared sour-dough with ¼ litre (scant ½ pint) of the lukewarm water and 4 tablespoons of the rye flour. Stir to form a smooth paste. Cover and prove overnight. On the following day mix in the other ingredients, except the oats, to form a cohesive dough. Turn out on to a floured board and pound and knead vigorously, adjusting the texture of the dough, if necessary, till smooth and elastic. Roll into a ball and dust with a little flour. Cover and prove for about 1½ hours. Shape into a large round loaf and place on a greased baking sheet which has been sprinkled with rolled oats. Bake at 200°C/400°F for 70–80 minutes.

SIEBENBÜRGENER GRIEBENBROT

250g (9oz) strong plain
    flour
250g (9oz) plain flour
¼ litre (½ pint) lukewarm
    water

125g (4½oz) sour-dough
10g (⅓oz) fresh yeast
100g (4oz) finely minced
    bacon fat
2 teaspoons salt

Sift the flour into a large bowl and press a well into the centre. Add a little of the water to the sour-dough and stir to make a smooth runny paste. Pour into the well and crumble the yeast into the sour-dough. Stir to dissolve, drawing in a little flour from the edges of the well. Cover the bowl and stand in a warm place to prove for about half an hour. Meanwhile fry the minced bacon fat till golden and drain on paper towels. Combine the flours and yeast sponge in the bowl, adding the remaining water and salt and mixing to a smooth dough. Turn out on to a floured board and knead vigorously for 10 minutes, then knead in the bacon shreds or *Grieben*. Form into a large loaf and place on a greased baking sheet. Prove briefly once again and bake at 230°C/450°F for 50–60 minutes.

POPPYSEED WHEEL

This decorative wheel-shaped bread is very attractive when laid directly on the table, accompanied either by unsalted butter and homemade jam for breakfast, or served as a first course with fresh *pâté maison*. Plan to make the wheel as large as possible, i.e. as large as your oven, or, if you have an understanding local baker, persuade him to allow you to use one of his large oven trays and oven.

Method
Prepare one quantity of French bread (p. 81). Allow the dough to prove once, and then punch it down and knead lightly. Divide it into four or five pieces for ease in handling and roll out the pieces into long thin ropes. This is best done on a large working area, such as the kitchen table, bringing a firm pressure to bear on the dough so that it will lengthen. Fashion one rope into as large a ring as possible and place it on a greased baking sheet, taking care not to pull the ring taut as it could distort during proving. Roll another rope into a circle which is somewhat smaller than the first, and place it inside the other on the baking sheet. With the remaining ropes weave spokes between the inner and outer rings, fastening the loose ends underneath the two circles by pinching the dough together. Cover the wheel and prove till light and puffy. Brush quickly with beaten egg and sprinkle with poppyseeds. Bake at 200°C/400°F for 15 minutes.

LAPP RIESKA

This bread is leavened through the use of baking powder and is shaped to make a wide, flat circle. It is traditionally made with barley flour but rye can be substituted instead. It is eaten hot, spread with butter.

250g (9oz) barley flour
¾ teaspoon salt
2 teaspoons baking powder
2 tablespoons melted butter

2 teaspoons sugar
approx. ¼ litre (½ pint)
single cream

Place the flour and salt in a bowl. Sift the baking powder over it. Stir in the melted butter, sugar and enough of the cream to make a smooth, soft dough. Flour the hands and roll the dough into a ball. Transfer to a greased baking sheet and press into as large a circle as the baking sheet will allow – the dough should not be more than 1cm (½in) thick. Prick with a fork and bake at 220°C/400°F for 10 minutes or till lightly browned. Serve in wedges.

RUSSIAN BLACK BREAD

This aromatic bread has a character all its own which has made it a favourite for those who value variety in their loaf. Black bread keeps well and develops its full flavour a day or two after baking.

45g (2½oz) fresh yeast
1 teaspoon sugar
½ litre (¾ pint) warm water
60g (2oz) butter
75ml (⅛ pint) molasses
75ml (⅛ pint) vinegar
30g (1oz) cooking
    chocolate
2 teaspoons instant coffee
2 teaspoons salt
2 teaspoons caraway seeds

2 teaspoons onion powder or
    1 tablespoon finely
    chopped onion
600g (1lb 6oz) rye flour
300g (11oz) wholemeal flour
100g (4oz) plain flour

Glaze
1 teaspoon cornflour
    dissolved in 75ml
    (⅛ pint) water

Cream the yeast with the sugar and dissolve in the warm water. Add the softened butter, molasses, vinegar, melted chocolate, coffee, salt, caraway seeds, onion powder and rye and wholemeal flour and proceed to work the ingredients with the hand till well combined. Adjust the moisture in the dough by adding all or part of the plain flour to make a stiff dough. Turn out on to a floured board and knead firmly for 10 minutes. Shape into a ball and place in a greased bowl, turning the dough so that it becomes coated with grease on all sides. Cover and prove till doubled in bulk. Punch down and knead again for 5 minutes. Divide into two parts and shape each into a log. Cover and prove till doubled in bulk. Bake at 200–220°C/400–425°F for about one hour or until the bases of the loaves sound hollow when tapped. Five minutes before the completion of baking, brush with the glaze.

BUTTERMILK AND MALT LOAF

Before the days of mechanization, mill-wheels turning at the edge of a briskly flowing stream were a common sight. Today they can still be seen in Germany and America, and the miller operating his own stone-mill can judge the texture of the meal he is grinding by lifting a handful into the air and letting it fall through his fingers. In ancient times stone-mills were operated by slaves or asses, and the sound of corn being continually ground was such an accepted part of the daily rhythm that its cessation could only signify desolation. In modern times Western man is once again favouring the stone-mill as a source of unbleached and coarser meals for bread baking.

150g (5½oz) cracked wheat
350ml (generous ½ pint)
   boiling water
40g (1½oz) fresh yeast
50g (2oz) brown sugar
a little lukewarm water
scant ¼ litre (½ pint) buttermilk

75g (2½oz) unsalted butter
1 tablespoon malt or
   3 tablespoons Ovaltine
1 tablespoon salt
300g (11oz) plain flour
300g (11oz) unbleached
   flour

Place the cracked wheat in a large bowl and pour the boiling water over it. Let stand for a good hour. Dissolve the yeast and brown sugar in a little lukewarm water, cover with a cloth and let it stand for 10 minutes. Heat the buttermilk and dissolve the butter, malt and salt in it. When the buttermilk has cooled to lukewarm, add to the yeast and sugar. Pour the liquid over the cracked wheat and stir well to break down any lumps. Beat in the flours a cup at a time and when the mixture becomes too stiff to beat, turn out on to a floured board and knead in the remaining flour or enough to make a soft but not sticky dough. Continue kneading for 10 minutes or till the dough is elastic. Gather into a ball and grease lightly with a little melted butter. Cover the dough and prove till doubled in bulk. Punch down and divide into two parts. Fill two greased loaf pans with the dough, cover and prove again till doubled in bulk. Brush with a little beaten egg and bake at 200–220°C/400–425°F for approximately 45 minutes or till the loaves are golden and make a hollow sound when tapped on their bases.

MOROCCAN ANISEED BREAD

Morocco is a country of brilliant sunshine, mosques, sand-coloured houses set at the edge of desert, and wonderful blooming trees such as the oleander and poinsettia, where a distinct Arab culture has been enriched and diversified by the influx of the Moors, Spanish, Romans and French. In Fès, the oldest of the royal cities, is found one of the world's most ancient universities and also the essence of the Moroccan cuisine with its couscous, made of crushed millet or rice, lamb and pigeon pies and rounds of sesame and aniseed bread.

600g (1lb 5oz) plain flour
60g (2oz) wholewheat flour
20g (⅔oz) fresh yeast
1 teaspoon sugar
2 teaspoons salt
⅛ litre (¼ pint) warm milk

⅜ litre (¾ pint) lukewarm water
1 tablespoon aniseed
1½ teaspoons sesame seeds
a little cornmeal

Place the flour in a bowl and press a well into the centre. Dissolve the yeast and sugar in a little lukewarm water and stand aside till the yeast starts to bubble. Dissolve the salt in the remaining milk and water and add to the yeast mixture. Pour into the flour well and combine the ingredients thoroughly to make a stiffish dough. Turn out on to a floured board and knead for 10 minutes. Incorporate the aniseed and sesame seeds in the dough by kneading gently once it is smooth and elastic. Divide the dough and shape each part into a ball. Cover with a cloth and let rest for 15 minutes. With oiled hands shape the dough into round loaves about a handspan in diameter, doming them a little in the centre. Dust a large baking sheet with a little cornmeal and place the loaves on it, leaving sufficient room for them to rise without touching each other. Prick the loaves with a fork at intervals round the outside of the loaf, cover with a damp cloth and prove till well risen. Dust with a little plain flour and bake at 220°C/425°F for 7 minutes and then reduce the temperature to 180°C/350°F and bake a further 36 minutes till the loaves are done.

AMERICAN PUMPKIN BREAD

This is a moist, warm-coloured bread which tastes a little sweet. As well as making the bread with pumpkin, curbis, squash or sweet potatoes can be substituted instead. Be careful to correct the dough for too much moisture during kneading, however, as the vegetables make for a sticky consistency.

30g (1oz) fresh yeast
75g (2½oz) sugar
3–4 tablespoons warm water
500g (1lb 2oz) plain flour
4–5 teaspoons salt

1 egg
75g (2½oz) melted butter
⅛ litre (¼ pint) in volume of
　mashed pumpkin
cream to glaze the loaf

Cream the yeast with a little sugar and dissolve in the warm water. Sift the flour and salt into a bowl and press a well into the centre. Beat the egg and combine with the melted butter. Add the yeast and butter mixtures to the flour together with the remaining sugar. Using a wooden spoon stir the ingredients briskly, gradually blending in the mashed pumpkin. Turn out on to a board and knead briefly till smooth. The dough will be soft but not too sticky. Cover with a cloth and prove till doubled in bulk. Punch down the dough and shape into a ball. Pinch off pieces of dough the size of a plum and roll into a smooth shape. Grease a tube pan and pile the balls into it, brushing each ball with a very little melted butter before fitting it into the pan. Be sure that the dough does not come further than two-thirds of the way up the tin. Cover and prove till well risen. Bake at 200°C/400°F for 45–55 minutes or until the loaf is done. Serve warm by pulling the pieces apart with the fingers.

SCOTTISH OATEN CAKES

Closely related to other oaten cakes of Celtic origin such as the Welsh siot and hara ceirch, the Scottish oatcake was once always baked on a griddle or bakestone. The cakes or, more aptly, rolls, are marked with a cross and served hot with herring and cheese or at tea time with butter and jam.

200g (7oz) oatmeal
100g (3½oz) plain flour
½ teaspoon baking powder
rolled oats

½ teaspoon salt
30g (1oz) melted butter
1½ tablespoons hot water

Mix all the dry ingredients together. Stir in the melted butter and then the hot water a little at a time to make a firm dough. Shape into a roll and divide into 8 or 10 pieces of equal size. Roll each piece into a ball and stack next to a board. Scatter the board with rolled oats flakes. Press each ball into the oats, flattening it out to make a thick cake. Turn the cake over and coat the other side with the oat flakes. With a razor blade or knife, make a cross on the top of each cake and transfer carefully to a greased baking sheet or griddle. Bake at 200–220°C/ 400–425°F for 15 minutes. Turn off the heat and leave the oatcakes a further 5 minutes in the oven till dry and light. Serve hot with butter, and herrings or barley broth.

GRANDMA BETSY LARSON'S SWEDISH RYE BREAD

50g (2oz) fresh yeast
1 teaspoon sugar
½ litre (¾ pint) warm water
500g (1lb 2oz) plain flour
4 tablespoons molasses
pinch baking soda

100g (4oz) melted butter
150g (5oz) brown sugar
2 teaspoons salt
400g (14oz) rye flour
aniseed

Dissolve the yeast and 1 teaspoon sugar in a little lukewarm water. Add the rest of the water and enough plain flour to make a soft sponge. Cover, and allow to stand till bubbly. Beat in molasses and a pinch of soda, then melted butter, brown sugar, salt and rye flour. If you are including the aniseed in the recipe – some people do not like the flavour – add at this stage. Work the ingredients with the hand, adding a little more plain flour if the dough seems too sticky. Turn out on to a floured board and knead for 10 minutes. Form into a ball and place in a greased bowl, turning the dough to coat all sides evenly. Prove till doubled in bulk, punch down, and knead lightly once again. Divide into two parts and place each in a greased bread pan. Cover the pans and prove till light and puffed. Bake at 200°C/400°F for about 40 minutes.

AUSTRALIAN DAMPER

In the days of early settlement in Australia where enormous distances had to be covered on foot or horseback, cooking and kitchen facilities were largely improvised. With perhaps the aid of a Dutch oven (an open iron box turned towards the fire), and a simple spit made of a long stout stick slung between two forked sticks on which the 'billy' or water container could be hung, bush cooks were expected to be able to cook a meal which would at least sustain the hearty appetites of drovers and travellers alike. Bread was ingeniously baked underground – a simple, unleavened loaf much like the scone, and called *damper*. This system of baking is found in the Eastern States of Northern America as well, where large quantities of clams are collected and baked under glowing coals in the sand.

In their book *Journey Among Men*, Jock Marshall and Russell Drysdale relate impressions gleaned while on a long ramble through the Australian Outback, including the 'mystical operation' of making good damper:

... 'You take flour and water ... Carefully you make a big mound of the flour, and in its centre you scoop a deep depression. Into this crater you pour enough water to form a small lake. Now you work the edges of the lake inwards until you have a big lump of firm, damp dough. This should be kneaded so that the air will be mechanically incorporated. This is a highly important part of the process ... shape the lump of aerated dough into a slab, not more than three inches thick.

Now is the time to rake the burning branches off the fire until only a bed of embers remains. A deep depression is scooped in the glowing charcoal, and into this the damper is dropped flat. Many bushmen allow the damper to remain like this for a few minutes; it "lets the outside get used to the heat" they say. Finally, clean smouldering coals are raked inwards and the damper is now covered.

After a suitable period (varying according to the size of the damper) some of the top embers are scraped away so that the damper can be tested with the point of a knife. This can be done more than once. At length, it sounds hollowish to the tap. Now it is golden brown in colour, and may be reverently disinterred. It smells like fresh heaven . . .'

Journey Among Men
JOCK MARSHALL AND RUSSELL DRYSDALE

500g (1 lb 2oz) plain flour
4 teaspoons baking powder
    (originally dampers were
    not made with any leaven
    at all)

1 teaspoon salt
60g (2oz) bacon or beef lard
¼ litre (½ pint) milk or water

Make a large fire of wood and kindling and let it blaze till a good bed of hot ash is formed. Blend all the ingredients above and have ready at the side of the fire. Rake away the ashes and scoop out a flat depression from the earth. Scatter some hot ash into the hole and lay the damper dough on it (if your heart is in your mouth at the thought of a true ash-damper crust to your loaf, wrap the dough in an old linen cloth). Rake the hot but not glowing ashes over the dough to cover it, and replace red embers on top of this. Leave for at least ½–¾ hour. In the meantime build up the fire close to where the damper is baking – but not on top of it – and bring some water to the boil. When it reaches boiling point, throw in some tea leaves and let steep till well drawn. Bush people hasten the drawing by taking hold of the billy, which is the round water container with bucket-like handle, and swinging it with a lightning movement over their heads. Drink the bush tea black with the damper.

CALIFORNIAN CHILLI
AND CORN BREAD (America)

Strung out along the west coast of America between Canada
and Mexico, California is a state of many races where in-
numerable cuisines intermingle. Once north of Tijuana the
traveller is in California, but he is still surrounded by all the
wonderful Mexican kitchen aromas of chillis, red hot peppers
and baking beans. Even as far north as Berkeley, he will be
regaled by crisp tortillas and, possibly, corn bread.

3–4 *tablespoons milk*	125g *(4½oz) grated cheese*
¼ *litre (½ pint) sour cream*	*such as Monterey Jack*
125g *(4½oz) melted butter*	*or Gouda*
2 *eggs*	125g *(4½oz) yellow*
2 *large cooked corn cobs*	*cornmeal (polenta)*
2 *teaspoons salt*	50–100g *(2–4oz) plain*
2–3 *finely chopped chillis or*	*flour*
1½ *teaspoons chilli powder*	3 *teaspoons baking powder*

Beat all the liquid ingredients till smooth. Pare the corn
from the cob and add to the liquid. Stir in the salt, chillis and
cheese. Sift the flours with the baking powder and gradually
blend into the mixture, adding enough flour to make a pour-
ing batter. Grease a casserole terra cotta or ceramic soufflé
dish and bake the bread at 190°C/375°F for about one hour.
Serve hot.

BRIOCHE À TÊTE (France)

There are many forms of brioche available in France: large
Brioches en Couronnes which are sold at Easter time,
brioches made with cheese, and large and small brioches à

têtes which are fluted and surmounted by a head or *tête*. They are very popular both at breakfast and at the afternoon *goûter*, and although it takes a little practice to learn how to turn out a perfect brioche, the sight of one of them on your morning or afternoon tea plate will surely encourage you to perfect the art of baking them. Remember that the brioche dough has a large proportion of butter in it, which becomes sticky during proving and kneading – the dough will therefore need to be chilled before it is used, and if it is required for breakfast, prepared the day before.

650g (1¼lb) plain flour
30g (1oz) fresh yeast
a little warm water
⅛ litre (¼ pint) warm milk
1 tablespoon sugar
2 teaspoons salt

250g (9oz) butter
5 eggs

Glaze
1 beaten egg

Sift the flour and set aside. Dissolve the yeast in a little warm water, then stir in the warm milk, sugar and salt. Beat in two cups of the flour, continuing to beat till blended. Now add the softened butter and beat vigorously till smooth. Add the eggs one at a time and the remaining flour. The dough will now seem to be fluid and sticky. Beat a further 10 minutes or until the dough becomes shiny and elastic – don't skimp on the beating because it is at this stage that an underbeaten brioche becomes a bad brioche. Now take hold of the dough firmly with both hands and lift it out of the bowl. Slap it down on a wooden surface, pick up again and continue this beating and slapping till the dough no longer sticks to the fingers. Return to a greased bowl, cover and prove till doubled in bulk. Stir with a spoon to collapse dough and place in the refrigerator for at least 4 hours or, preferably, overnight. When ready to use, divide the dough into fifteen equal pieces. If you are using brioche pans, keep only enough dough out of the refrigerator as can be baked at one time. Pinch off a little dough from the ball to be shaped, reserving it for the head. Shape the remainder into a smooth ball and place in a greased brioche tin. With a sharp knife, bore a hole in the dome of the brioche. Roll the small piece of reserved dough into a tear-shaped peg and insert into the incision in the brioche, making sure that the *tête* is secure, and flatten a little as well. Cover the brioche pans with greaseproof paper and prove till the brioches are risen. Brush with beaten egg and bake at 200°C/400°F for 20 minutes.

BRIOCHE MOUSSELINE

This brioche is baked in a plain, cylindrical mould, the height of which is further extended by tying a collar of greased paper round the top of the tin. Butter the mould and fill to two-thirds its height with refrigerated brioche dough as given in the recipe for Brioches à Têtes. Leave in the pan till the dough is risen to the top, and bake at 200°C/400°F for 30–40 minutes, or till the brioche gives off a hollow sound when tapped.

CORNSTICKS (America)

Early American settlers learned the use of cornmeal in baking bread from the North American Red Indians, and since colonial days cornflour has been an important and characteristic inclusion in the American and neighbouring Mexican diet. To make the cornsticks you will need a cast-iron cornstick mould which is obtainable from stores specialising in kitchen equipment. Make sure that the mould is sizzling hot before filling the compartments with batter. As most moulds usually make only 6–8 sticks at a time, it will be necessary to bake the cornsticks in batches, greasing the mould before each new addition of batter.

bacon fat
175g (6oz) plain flour
175g (6oz) yellow
   cornmeal (polenta)
3 teaspoons baking powder

2 teaspoons salt
6og (2oz) melted butter
¼ litre (½ pint) mixed milk
   and buttermilk
2 eggs

Render the bacon fat by frying gently till all the liquid fat has been drawn out. Reserve. Sift the flours, baking powder and salt into a bowl. Gradually beat in the melted butter, milk and eggs to make a smooth batter without any lumps. Heat the cornstick mould till it is very hot and brush each compartment with the reserved bacon fat. Fill each section almost to the rim and bake in a hot (200°C/400°F) oven for 20 minutes or till brown and puffy. Remove from the mould at once.

JONNYCAKES

These little flour cakes seem to be irrevocably connected with travelling, hence their name, 'Journey Cakes'. Although they are best known from the colonial times in America and Australia, it was an ancient race indeed which first discovered that cornflour made a light and therefore admirably portable type of bread. In Australia, the jonnycake was the swagman's main sustenance as he travelled the roads on foot, all his possessions in the *swag* tied to a stick and borne over his shoulder. The following quotation comes from a swaggy's song in which the swaggy contentedly confesses to being the jonnycake's creator.

> 'With me little white flour bag sittin' on the stump,
> Me little tea and sugar bag lookin' nice and plump,
> A little fat codfish just off the hook,
> And four little jonnycakes,
> A credit to the cook!'

1 *egg*	30g *(1oz) melted butter*
¼ *litre (½ pint) or less milk*	175g *(6oz) cornflour**
½ *teaspoon salt*	175g *(6oz) plain flour*
a little sugar	2 *teaspoons baking powder*

Beat the egg, milk, salt, sugar and melted butter till smooth. Sift the flours and baking powder together twice. Beat the flour into the liquid a little at a time, and continue beating till the mixture is smooth. Spoon into greased patty tins and bake at 220°C/425°F till golden – about 20 minutes. The jonnycakes can also be cooked in the traditional way on a hot greased griddle or in a heavy frying pan. They should be crusty on the outside and soft inside. Serve hot, pulling them gently apart with the fingers before buttering.

* Jonnycakes can be made with all plain flour if preferred.

LEFSE

Lefse originated in the far north of Europe – some say in Finland, others in Iceland. They are unusual in that no leavening is used, the result being a flat bread. In the compiling of this book I have noticed that leavening of any sort seems to be indigenous to the heart of Europe, from where it was carried to the New World when colonization of Africa, the Americas and Australia began. If you imagine the heart of Europe to be the centre of leavened breads, you will find that they become less and less frequent and known the further you move away from the centre. Thus, such fringe areas as Iceland, Turkey, Greece, Israel, Morocco, and even Portugal and Ireland have very few leavened forms of bread. In Mexico the tortilla is just as popular as bread, and in Asia – with the exception of a few breads such as Nan – leavened bread as we know it is unknown.

1 *tablespoon butter*	½ *teaspoon salt*
¼ *litre (½ pint) sour milk or buttermilk*	500g *(1 lb 2oz) flour*

Melt the butter and add to the milk. Using the hand, gradually incorporate the salt and flour into the milk adding a little more milk if the dough seems too stiff. Turn out on to a floured board and knead briefly. Allow the dough to rest a little. Form into a roll and cut into slices. Roll out each slice into a thin round pancake shape. Brown lightly on a griddle and stack the lefses on top of each other. Before serving, spread with butter and sprinkle with brown sugar.

LIGHT PUMPERNICKEL

30g (1oz) fresh yeast
¼ litre (scant ½ pint) warm
  water
1 teaspoon sugar
½ litre (¾ pint) warm milk
50g (2oz) butter

2 tablespoons molasses
1 beaten egg
½ tablespoon salt
1kg (2¼lb) rye flour
2 tablespoons caraway seeds

Dissolve the yeast in the water together with one teaspoon sugar. Heat the milk and dissolve the butter in it. Allow to cool to lukewarm, then stir in the molasses, beaten egg, salt and yeast mixture. Add a quarter of the flour and the caraway seeds and beat until smooth. Cover the batter and leave to rise for 30 minutes. Stir in half the remaining flour, cover and let rise a further 30 minutes. Now add the rest of the flour, or enough to make a dough which is not sticky, turn out on to a floured board and knead for 8–10 minutes. Shape into two oval loaves and roll these in floured tea towels so that they will maintain their shape. Prove till risen. Unwrap, and transfer the loaves to greased oven sheets. Bake at 200°C/400°F for about 40 minutes. A few minutes before the end of the baking time, brush with milk to glaze.

YORKSHIRE PUDDING (England)

There was a time when every roast joint was served with
Yorkshire Pudding. Perhaps it first made its appearance in
Yorkshire as a substitute for potatoes when they were scarce
or expensive. With the cost of living rising so sharply, and
particularly where vegetables are concerned, perhaps the
twentieth century Sunday Roast will see a return of this
magic pudding.

300g (11oz) plain flour
1 teaspoon salt
200ml (⅓ pint) milk

200ml (⅓ pint) cream
4 eggs

Sift the flour and salt together. Stir in the milk and cream,
and beat with a whisk till smooth. Beat the eggs and add to
the batter. Beat till very smooth. About half an hour before
the roast is finished, drain off a little of the roast fat into a
separate dish and return it to the oven to reheat. Spoon the
batter into the sizzling fat and bake alongside the meat till
golden. Drain and serve with the meat and baked vegetables.

GEORGIAN KHACHAPURI (Russia)

Georgia is one of Russia's southernmost states, perched at
the foot of the Caucases between the Caspian and Black seas.
It is an area where Armenian, Turkish and Persian delicacies
such as halva, shashlyk and baklava give way to the more
northern delights, such as the little pies known as pirozhki
and borsch, not to mention the heavy black peasant bread of
the Ukraine.

500g (1 lb 2oz) flour
15g (½oz) fresh yeast

50g (2oz) sugar
⅛ litre (¼ pint) milk

100g *(4oz) butter*
2 *eggs*
1 *teaspoon salt*

Filling
650g *(1¼lb) Tilsiter* or
   Danish Havarti cheese

1 *tablespoon Blue Vein*
   cheese
60g *(2oz) melted butter*
pepper and salt
¼ *teaspoon ground*
   coriander
1 *large egg*

Sift the flour into a bowl and press a well into the centre.
Cream the yeast with a little of the sugar and dissolve in a
little lukewarm milk. Cover the yeast and let it rest for a few
minutes. Scald the milk, remove from the heat and cut the
butter into small pieces and drop into the hot milk. Allow to
cool to lukewarm and then beat in the eggs, salt and remaining sugar. Combine with the yeast sponge and pour into the
well in the flour. Beat the mixture briskly till it forms a cohesive dough, then turn out on to a floured board and adjust
the amount of flour or moisture in the dough to make a soft
but not sticky dough. Continue to knead till smooth and
elastic. Cover the dough and prove till double in bulk. Punch
down and knead lightly again, and then roll out to a circle
roughly 50cm (20in) in diameter. Fold the dough over the
rolling pin and lift on to a greased pie dish or spring form.
Spread the dough out so that the edges fall over the rim of
the dish. Cover the plate and let the dough rest while you
prepare the filling. Grate the Tilsiter cheese and combine
with the other filling ingredients. Spread the mixture over
the dough, heaping it towards the centre. Fold the dough
flaps over the cheese filling, pleating them at regular intervals. Twist the ends into a decorative knot or rose in the
middle. Prove briefly, brush with beaten egg and bake at
190°C/375°F for 1 hour or until golden.

FOCASSIA (Italy)

Focassia is similar to pizza in that it is baked in flat rectangles for a short period in a very hot oven. This recipe produces an aromatic bread with the flavour of onions and the perfume of garlic.

1 *quantity of dough prepared from 250g (9oz) flour using Basic White Bread recipe (see page 23)*
3–4 *tablespoons warm milk mixed with 1 tablespoon melted butter*

olive oil
1 *finely chopped onion*
3 *large garlic cloves cut in slivers*

After the dough has risen once, punch down and knead the milk and melted butter into it. Roll out thinly to a large rectangle about 1½cm (½in) thick and dribble olive oil sparingly over the surface of the dough. With a pointed knife insert garlic slivers at random over the Focassia and sprinkle with the finely chopped onion. Prove till puffy and light and bake at 220°C/425°F till golden – 15–20 minutes. Serve hot and remove the garlic before bringing to the table.

CORNISH PASTIES (England)

300g *(11oz) flour*
15g *(½oz) fresh yeast*
¾ *cup warm milk*
30g *(1oz) melted butter*
1½ *teaspoons salt*
1 *beaten egg white*

Filling
¼ *cup finely chopped onion*
200g *(7oz) sausage meat*
½ *cup diced, cooked carrot*
½ *cup diced, cooked turnip*
½ *cup diced, cooked potato*
1 *teaspoon salt*
pepper

Sift the flour into a basin, and press a well into the centre. Dissolve the yeast in a little of the warm milk and pour into the flour well. Stir to make a paste and then set aside for 10 minutes to prove. Add the melted butter, salt and remaining milk to the flour, and mix to a smooth consistency. Turn out on to a floured board and knead till elastic. Cover and prove till double in bulk. Punch down the dough and knead lightly for a minute. Divide the dough into eight equal parts and roll each part into a circle about 20–25cm (8–10in) in diameter. Place a little of the filling on one half of the circle, fold the other half over the filling, bringing the edges neatly together. Moisten the edges with a little egg white and press firmly together to seal. Allow to prove in a warm place for 30 minutes, then slit the top of the pasty to allow steam to escape during baking. Bake at 200–220°C/400–425°F for 15–20 minutes.

To prepare the filling
Brown the onion and sausage meat, and cook gently for 5 minutes. Add the remaining vegetables and season with pepper and salt. If necessary, bind with a little flour. Allow to cool to lukewarm before filling pasties.

Chapter Five

'BREAD AND HONEY'

RECIPES FOR SWEET TEA BREADS

HONEY AND RUM TEA LOAF (England)

'Stand's the church clock at ten to three?
And is there honey still for tea?'

RUPERT BROOKE

From an alien land, RUPERT BROOKE wrote with longing
and nostalgia for his beloved England, and in particular of
Cambridgeshire. Even today one can follow his path out of
Cambridge, through Trumpington and along the balmy lanes
to Grantchester, that 'lovely hamlet' where he is still remem-
bered as being one of England's most lyrical poets.

125g (4½oz) raisins
2 tablespoons rum
500g (1lb 2oz) wholemeal
 flour
500g (1lb 2oz) plain flour
1 egg
½ litre (¾ pint) warm milk

75ml (⅛ pint) honey
50g (2oz) unsalted butter
1½ teaspoons salt
30g (1oz) fresh yeast
a little sugar
gelatine glaze (see p. 21)

Soak the raisins in rum overnight. Place the flours in a large
bowl and press a well into the centre of the flour. Crack the
egg into the well. Scald the milk, remove from the heat and
add the honey, diced butter and salt to it. Allow to cool till
lukewarm. Cream the yeast with a little sugar and dissolve
in the lukewarm milk and honey. Pour into the flour and
work the ingredients till they form a cohesive dough. Turn

out on to a floured board and knead till smooth and elastic. Gradually knead in the raisins and any rum which has not been taken up during soaking, adding a little more flour if the dough is too sticky. Gather into a ball and grease lightly on all sides. Cover and prove till doubled in bulk. Punch down and knead very briefly. Divide the dough into two parts and place in greased loaf pans. Cover and prove till doubled in bulk. Bake at 200°C/400°F for 40–50 minutes. Allow to cool a little and brush with gelatine or other glaze.

The honey loaf is best served toasted and spread with unsalted butter and honey.

APFELKUCHEN (Germany)

500g (1lb 2oz) plain flour
salt
100g (4oz) sugar
40g (1½oz) fresh yeast
¼ litre (½ pint) warm milk
60g (2oz) butter
grated rind of ½ lemon

Filling
1kg (2¼lb) apples

1 teaspoon butter
lemon juice to taste
85g (3oz) sugar
100g (4oz) sultanas
3 tablespoons rum
¼ teaspoon cinnamon
100g (4oz) slivered almonds
1 egg white
1 egg

First prepare the dough. Sift the flour, salt and sugar into a bowl and press a well into the centre. Cream the yeast with one teaspoon of sugar and dissolve in the warm milk. Cover and allow to rest a little. Melt the butter and cool to lukewarm. Add to the milk and yeast and pour the liquid into the well in the flour. Grate the lemon rind over the well and then combine the ingredients with the hand till the dough is cohesive. Turn out on to a floured board and knead till smooth and elastic. Gather into a ball and grease lightly with a little butter. Cover the dough and prove till double in bulk.

Meanwhile, prepare the filling. Peel the apples and cut into thick slices, stamping out the core with an apple-corer. Poach them gently in 3–4 tablespoons of water with a small knob of butter and the lemon juice and 85g(3oz)sugar till tender – approximately 6 minutes. Remove from the heat and allow to cool to lukewarm. Stir in the sultanas, rum, cinnamon and almonds. When the dough has risen, punch down and knead lightly. Roll out to a thickness which will fit a round flan case with a removable bottom, reserving enough dough to make a lid for the cake. Line the base and walls of a greased flan case with the dough, letting the edges hang over the rim. Spread the apple filling over the dough and then fold in the edges over it. Roll out the remaining dough to form a circle the size of the flan case, and lay it over the apple filling. Seal with a little egg white at the edges, pressing them together gently. With the apple corer cut a vent in the centre of the lid, and prick the surface of the applecake with a fork. Cover with a cloth and prove for about 30 minutes or until the dough seems light. Brush with beaten egg and bake at 200°C/400°F for about 30 minutes. Dust with a little castor sugar.

SHORTBREAD PETTICOAT TAILS
(Scotland)

Scottish shortbread is eaten in all Western countries, and whether it is bought in round tins decorated with gay tartans – glimpses of the Highlands – or made at home in preparation for Christmas, it is certain to disappear within the twinkling of an eye once placed on the table. Story has it that the name 'petticoat tail' originates from the cut of seventeenth century petticoats.

600g (1lb 5oz) plain flour	500g (1lb 2oz) unsalted
200g (7oz) castor sugar	butter

Sift the flour and sugar together and quickly rub the ice-cold butter into it. Roll out the dough to 2 circles approximately 30cm (12in) in diameter and prick all over with a fork. Transfer to a greased baking sheet and press intersecting lines, marking triangles, into the dough with the back of a knife. Pinch or slash the outer edge of the shortbread in a decorative pattern and bake at 190°C/375°F for 25 minutes or until delicately browned. When serving, break into triangular pieces. Shortbread can be stored for months in airtight jars.

SAVARIN AUX CERISES (France)

No book on breads would be complete without the inclusion of savarin – known also as *baba* – that delightful offspring of cake and bread, made particularly delicious by being soaked in liqueurs. The savarin is served either as a dessert, or with coffee, and is invariably accompanied by its own syrup, fruits or Chantilly cream. This recipe pairs the savarin with cherries in the style of Montmorency, but it is equally possible to prepare it with any other fruit.

1kg (2¼lb) Morello
  cherries
sugar
500g (1lb 2oz) flour
20g (⅔oz) fresh yeast
⅛ litre (¼ pint) warm milk
8 eggs

2 tablespoons sugar
1½ teaspoons salt
375g (13oz) butter
kirsch
¼ litre (½ pint) double cream
2 tablespoons cherry brandy

First prepare the cherries. Place the stoned cherries in a bowl and sprinkle them with sugar. Add twelve of the sherry stones, cracked and tied in a muslin bag. If the stones have not been retained add a dash of bitter almond essence. Allow the fruit to stand till the sugar starts to draw out the cherry juice. Simmer the cherries in their own juice for seven minutes. Cool.

Prepare the dough. Sift the flour into a large bowl and press a well into the centre. Crumble the yeast into the well and add one teaspoon of the sugar. Add a little of the warm milk and stir to make a paste. Crack the eggs into the paste and work with the fingertips till smooth. Cover the bowl and prove for 20 minutes. Now add the remaining milk, sugar, and salt and, working with the hands rub in the butter. Beat the ingredients with a wooden spoon till they are completely incorporated. Place the dough in a greased Savarin or ring mould, filling it to two-thirds of its height. Cover and prove till the dough almost reaches the top of the mould. Bake at 200°C/400°F for 40–45 minutes. Cool the Savarin in the mould before turning out. Soak the cake in the cherry juice which has formed while the cherries were cooking. Sprinkle the Savarin with plenty of kirsch liqueur. Place the drained cherries in the centre of the Savarin, reserving some for decoration. Beat the cream and flavour with cherry brandy. Pile this on top of the cherries and decorate with the reserved cherries.

BARA BRITH (Wales)

'Evans the Death, the undertaker, laughs high and aloud in his sleep and curls up his toes as he sees, upon waking fifty years ago, snow lie deep on the goosefield behind the sleeping house; and he runs out into the field where his mother is making welsh-cakes in the snow, and steals a fistful of snowflakes and currants and climbs back to bed to eat them cold and sweet under the warm, white clothes . . .'

Under Milkwood – DYLAN THOMAS

Whether Dylan Thomas had Bara Brith in mind when he wrote of Evans the Death's dream I do not know, but every Welshman is familiar with this rich, sweet bread of their homeland.

30g (1oz) fresh yeast
1 teaspoon sugar
⅛ litre (¼ pint) warm milk
11g (4oz) butter or lard
500g (1lb 2oz) plain flour
125g (4½oz) brown sugar
¼ teaspoon mixed spice

½ teaspoon salt
30g (1oz) mixed peel
1 egg
125g (4½oz) sultanas
125g (4½oz) currants
110g (4oz) raisins

Cream the yeast, sugar and a little of the warm milk together, and allow to stand a little. Cut the fat into the flour,
then mix in the sugar, spice, salt and peel. Press a well into
the centre of the flour mixture and spoon the egg, yeast and
milk into it. Work the dough with the hand, adding enough
warm milk to make a soft but not sticky dough. Turn out on
to a floured board and knead for 8 minutes. Now incorporate
the other fruits into the dough. Cover and prove till double
in bulk. Knead lightly once again, roll into a loaf and press
into a rectangular, greased baking tin. Prove a second time
till double in bulk. Bake at 190°C/375°F for approximately
1–1½ hours. While still hot, glaze with thin vanilla icing.

HAZELNUT CHOCOLATE COFFEE CAKE

500g (1lb 2oz) plain flour
pinch salt
30g (1oz) fresh yeast
100g (4oz) sugar
⅛ litre (¼ pint) warm milk
1 egg
75g (2½oz) butter
vanilla icing

Filling
200g (7oz) ground or
    finely chopped hazelnuts
150g (5oz) sugar
3 tablespoons cocoa
6–7 tablespoons milk

Sift the flour and salt into a bowl. Make a well in the centre.
Cream the yeast with a little sugar and dissolve in the milk.
Crack the egg into the well and shave the softened butter

over the flour. Pour the yeast and milk into the well and combine all the ingredients thoroughly. Turn out on to a floured board and knead till very smooth and elastic. Roll the dough into a ball and grease lightly. Return the dough to the bowl and prove till doubled in bulk. Punch down the dough and knead lightly once again. Roll out to a rectangle measuring about 30 × 12cm (12 × 5in). Combine the hazelnuts, sugar, cocoa and milk and mix to a paste. Spread the paste over the dough and roll up, starting at the long side of the rectangle. Cut the roll into nine slices. Grease a loose-bottomed cake tin and place one roll in the centre of it, with the cut side uppermost. Taper the other slices so that they fit round the centrepiece like cake segments, leaving a little room between each slice to allow for expansion. Prove briefly and bake at 190–200°C/375–400°F for 40–45 minutes or until golden. Cool for 10 minutes in the form, remove and brush sparingly with vanilla icing.

MUFFINS (England)

The classical English muffin is deceptively simple in its make-up. Although it is quick to prepare and serve, which makes it a favourite for breakfast, it is nonetheless easier to make badly than well. To achieve a good result, bake the muffins in special iron muffin tins in a very hot oven, and beat the mixture quickly – it will look lumpy but the resulting texture will be tender. There are hundreds of variations on muffins using nuts, jam, dried and fresh fruits. At the end of the recipe a list of suggested nuts and fruits is given: they can all be added to the dough before baking, but if the fruit is juicy, add a little extra flour and baking powder.

250g (9oz) plain flour
½ teaspoon salt
60g (2oz) sugar
1 teaspoon baking powder

1 egg
60g (2oz) melted butter
¼ litre (½ pint) milk

Sift the flour, salt, sugar and baking powder twice to combine and aerate thoroughly. Press a well into the centre of
the flour. Beat the egg and butter together and combine with
the milk. Pour into the well in the flour all at once and, using
a wooden spoon, stir very briefly so that the ingredients are
just moistened – 12–15 strokes. Fill the greased muffin cups
to two-thirds their height. Bake at 220°C/425°F for 20–25
minutes or till browned. Serve with marmalade and butter
while still hot.

Variations
Oranges, lemons, red and black fresh currants, raspberries,
blueberries, figs, blackberries, dates, peaches, pears, bananas.
Walnuts, pecans, monkey nuts, almonds. Cinnamon, nutmeg,
cardamom, and tropical fruits such as mangoes, guavas,
passion fruit. Honey and jams.

SALLY LUNN (England)

This famous Bath cake dates from the eighteenth century
when, allegedly, a young girl from Somerset devised the cake
which was later to bear her name. Others argue that this
yeast cake was originally a native of France, 'Sally Lunn'
being an etymological derivation of 'sol et Lune'. If the cake
is British, it is certainly not typical, either in its shape, which
is hollow and domed, nor in the fact that it is traditionally
served with cream, a habit which one has come to associate
with countries on the other side of the Channel.

30g (1oz) fresh yeast	125g (4½oz) butter
125g (4½oz) sugar	3 eggs
a little warm water	600g (1lb 5oz) flour
175ml (¼–⅓ pint) warm milk and cream mixed	1 teaspoon salt

Dissolve the yeast, together with one teaspoon of the sugar in
the water. Combine with the milk and cream mixture.

Cream the butter and remaining sugar; beat the eggs and add to the creamed butter. Sift the flour and salt together and add to the butter alternately with yeast liquid. Beat vigorously with a wooden spoon till the mixture develops bubbles under its surface. Turn into a buttered bowl, cover and prove till double in bulk. Beat once again, and turn into a well-buttered and floured continental ring mould or a ring mould with high walls. Prove again till risen, and bake at a moderate temperature (190°C/375°F) till a straw inserted in the middle of the cake comes away clean.

SCONES (England)

Scones are a delight to every British soul. It is also a well-known fact that they are never made well by a young cook. Be that as it may, if served in the Devonshire manner with clotted or whipped cream and berry jam, even a child can produce scones to please the most hardened palate.

300g (11oz) plain flour
2 teaspoons sugar
½ teaspoon bicarbonate of soda
good pinch of cream of tartar
½ teaspoon salt

60g (2oz) butter (icy cold)
approx. 3–4 tablespoons milk or half milk, half sour cream
1 egg or milk for glaze
30g (1oz) butter

Sift all the dry ingredients together twice. Shave the 60g (2oz) butter into the flour, and rub in with the fingertips till the flour resembles coarse meal. Add just enough of the milk or a little more to form a cohesive dough. Gather into a ball and transfer to floured board. Press out the dough to a thickness of about 2cm (¾in). Fold in two and gently press out again. Cut into 9 pieces with a drinking glass or knife and place close together on a greased baking sheet. If the scones are not close together they will not rise as well. Brush with egg or milk, and divide the 30g (1oz) butter into 9 pieces.

Place each dot of butter in the centre of a scone and bake at 200°C/400°F for 15–20 minutes.

ZWETSCHGENBAATZ
Plum Cake (Germany)

This recipe comes from Franconia, which is the northern part of Bavaria. It is the homeland of beer steins and hearty beer, of *Klöße* or dumplings, caraway seeds and garlic, and the delicate white wine known as *Franken Wein* which is bottled in flat round bottles and prized amongst wine connoisseurs throughout the world.

The word *Zwetschgen* means plums, but the zwetschge is the special cooking plum which is elongated, firm and small, and the skin a deep red colour. Each summer when the plums ripen, the Frankonian housewife prepares generous quantities of plum cake to be served with coffee and heaped, whipped cream. Cooked for a long time with sugar, the zwetschgen also make an aromatic jam known as *Pflaumenmuss* which is almost black in colour and of a rich flavour.

⅛ litre (¼ pint) milk
20g (⅔oz) fresh yeast
300g (11oz) plain flour
2 tablespoons sugar

2 eggs
4 tablespoons breadcrumbs
1kg (2¼lb) stoned red plums
2–3 tablespoons oil

Heat the milk to lukewarm, and crumble the yeast into it, together with one teaspoon sugar. Stir the mixture till it is dissolved, and leave it to stand a little. Sift the flour on to a board, and make a well in the centre. Scatter the sugar round the outside of the well, and crack the eggs into the well. Break the egg yolks with a fork and pour the yeast and milk on top of them. Working with the fingers, gradually mix the liquid into the flour till it becomes a smooth dough. Roll the dough into a ball, cover it, and allow to prove for an hour. Roll out the dough to a thin rectangle the size of your largest baking sheet, puckering the edges a little so that they are somewhat raised. Scatter the breadcrumbs over the dough, and lay the stoned, quartered plums thickly on top. Cover the cake and allow it to prove till puffy and light. Bake at 200°C/400°F for 30 minutes. As soon as the *Baatz* is taken from the oven, sprinkle it liberally with sugar – this not only sweetens the cake, but also changes the plum juice liberated by baking to syrup.

KUGELHUPF

As mentioned earlier, the dividing line between 'cake' and 'bread' is often a very fine one. In days gone by the wealthy could afford to mix eggs and sugar into their bread at random, whereas for the poor this was a privilege to be enjoyed only on feast days, or perhaps not at all. Thus 'bread' became 'festival bread' or 'cake' as our forefather's standard of living rose.

'Kugelupf or Suglhupf (Alsatian pastry) – It is said that Queen Marie Antoinette was very fond of this pastry, which contributed a great deal to the fashion in her day for sweets made from risen dough. These were no longer made, as they had been until the middle of the eighteenth century, with leaven but with barm (brewer's yeast), which had been in use for a very long time in Austria and Poland.

Some authorities, however, believe that it was Carême who popularised this pastry in Paris, when he established himself as a pastry cook.'

LAROUSSE – *Gastronomique*

30g *(1oz) fresh yeast*
90g *(3oz) fine sugar*
½ cup *warm water*
500g *(1lb 2oz) plain flour*
200g *(7oz) butter*
1½ teaspoons *salt*

6 *eggs*
50g *(2oz) currants*
1 tablespoon *grated lemon peel*
½ cup *flaked almonds*

Dissolve the yeast with the sugar in the warm water, cover and allow to prove. Divide the flour equally between two bowls. Cut the butter into one of the bowls of flour, then mix in the salt and the eggs, one at a time beating vigorously with a wooden spoon between each addition. To this mixture add alternately the proven yeast liquid and the remaining bowl of flour. Beat again with the wooden spoon till the dough is elastic, and then add the currants and grated lemon peel. Gather the dough into a ball and dust it lightly with flour. Cover and allow to prove till double in bulk. Grease a kugelhupf mould and sprinkle half the almonds into it. Place half the risen dough in the mould and scatter the remaining almonds over its surface. Press the remaining dough lightly on to the almonds and then cover the Kugelhupf and allow to prove till risen. Bake at 200°C/400°F for 35–45 minutes. Serve with coffee.

HUNGARIAN SOUR CREAM COFFEE CAKE

30g (1oz) fresh yeast
⅛ litre (¼ pint) warm water
200g (7oz) butter
6 egg yolks
¼ litre (½ pint) or less sour
  cream
600g (1lb 5 oz) plain flour
½ teaspoon salt
125g (4½oz) sugar
apricot jam for glaze
icing sugar

Filling
225g (8oz) cream or
  cottage cheese
125g (4½oz) sugar
2 eggs
1 teaspoon vanilla essence
grated rind of 1 lemon

Cream the yeast with one teaspoon sugar and dissolve in the warm water. Melt the butter and allow to cool a little, then beat into the egg yolks and sour cream. Sift the flour, salt and sugar together twice. Gradually blend the sour cream and egg yolk mixture into the flour, and then stir in the yeast and water. Beat briskly till the dough is smooth. Turn out on to a floured board and knead for about 5 minutes till the dough is elastic. Roll into a ball and grease lightly with a little butter. Cover and prove till double in bulk. Meanwhile, prepare the cheese filling by beating the cream cheese till it is light and blending in successively the remaining sugar, eggs, vanilla and lemon rind.

Punch down the risen dough and knead lightly. Roll out to a circle about 40 cm (16in) in diameter and drape the dough over a greased ring mould, letting the dough fall over the rim of the mould. Fill the ring with the cheese filling, and then fold and pleat the dough on the outside so that it covers the filling. Slit a star-shaped incision in the dough resting over the chimney of the ring mould and fold the four corners of dough over the filling as well. In this way the filling will be completely encased by dough. Cover, and prove till the cake is well risen. Bake at 190°C/375°F for about 45 minutes or until golden. Test to see if the cake is done by pushing a straw into the centre – if it comes away clean, the cheese filling inside is set. Cool. To make the glaze, heat apricot jam and strain. Brush over cake. When set, and just before serving, sprinkle with icing sugar.

EAST COAST PRUNE BREAD (America)

Prune bread is a traditional American fruit loaf from the East Coast. The following recipe can be varied by substituting dried apricots, persimmons or pears for prunes.

200g (7oz) flour
2 teaspoons cinnamon
1 teaspoon baking powder
1 teaspoon baking soda
75g (2½oz) wholemeal flour
6 tablespoons butter
⅛ litre (¼ pint) honey

2 eggs
¼ teaspoon vanilla essence
grated rind of one lemon
100–150g (4–6oz) chopped, cooked prunes
⅛ litre (¼ pint) sour cream

Sift the dry ingredients together into a bowl and stir in the wholemeal flour. Cream the butter and honey and then beat in the eggs and vanilla and lemon rind. Toss the chopped prunes in the bowl of flour till coated with flour and then fold in the honey and egg mixture alternately with the sour cream. Grease a loaf pan and fill with the batter. Bake at 180°C/350°F for about 1 hour or until a straw, stuck into the centre of the prune bread comes away clean.

WAFFLES

To make waffles you will need a special waffle iron, as this is the only way to give the waffle its characteristic honey-combed surface.

250g (9oz) plain flour	½ teaspoon sugar
¼ teaspoon salt	½ litre milk
15g (½oz) fresh yeast	60g (2oz) butter
2–3 eggs	

Sift the flour and salt into a bowl. Cream the yeast and sugar. Heat the milk and dissolve the butter in it. Allow to cool to lukewarm and add the creamed yeast. Stir to dissolve. Using a whisk, gradually beat in the flour and continue beating till smooth. Cover the bowl and set aside in a warm place for about half an hour. Grease the waffle iron with butter and heat till the butter is sizzling. Bake the waffles one at a time and serve hot. They can be served buttered, with ice cream, whipped cream, any syrup such as maple, caramel, or raspberry or chocolate sauce.

CARDAMOM PLAIT (Norway)

Throughout the Scandinavian countries cardamom is a very popular spice in bread-making. The cardamom seeds are harvested by hand from the parent plant, ginger, and command a high price on the world market.

450g (1lb) plain flour
¾ teaspoon cardamom
75g (2½oz) sugar
20g (⅔oz) fresh yeast
warm water
½ teaspoon salt

⅛ litre (¼ pint) warm milk
1 egg
60g (2oz) butter
milk for glaze
pink vanilla icing

Sift the flour and cardamom into a bowl and press a well into the centre. Cream a little of the sugar with the yeast and dissolve it in warm water. Sprinkle the salt, and remaining sugar over the flour. Pour the dissolved yeast into the warm milk and stir thoroughly, then add to the flour in the bowl. Crack the egg into the well and shave the butter over the flour. Using a wooden spoon beat the mixture thoroughly until all the ingredients are thoroughly combined. Turn the dough out on to a floured board and knead for about 5 minutes. Gather into a ball and place in a greased bowl, turning the ball to coat it with grease. Cover and prove till doubled in bulk. Punch down and knead lightly. Divide into three equal portions. Roll each part into a rope and then plait the three strands loosely. Lift on to a greased baking sheet, cover and prove till risen. Brush with milk and bake at 200°C/400°F till golden – about 25 minutes. While still warm, trickle icing over the cardamom plait.

IRISH SODA BREAD

Think of Ireland, and one sees green hills and fields studded with horses and white-washed farm houses. Think of her cuisine, and a strange concoction of whiskey, potatoes and soda bread comes to mind. Soda bread is certainly ancient and in country farmhouses was traditionally baked in an iron pot slung over a peat fire.

500g (1lb 2oz) plain flour   1 teaspoon baking powder
1 teaspoon salt   ⅛ litre (¼ pint) buttermilk

Sift the flour, salt and baking powder together twice. Gradually blend in the buttermilk, adding more or less as needed. The dough should be cohesive and able to be shaped. Gather into a ball and shape into a round loaf. Place on a greased baking sheet, and, using a razor blade, mark a cross on the loaf to divide it into quarters or *farls*. Bake at 200°C/400°F for 40–45 minutes or until golden. Serve hot with unsalted butter.

CHELSEA BUNS (England)

Once known only in London where they originated, the sweet coil of the Chelsea Bun is now an international favourite, and can be seen in any baker's window alongside its counterpart, the Bath Bun.

280g (10oz) plain flour   1 teaspoon mixed spice
½ teaspoon salt   3 tablespoons currants
15g (½oz) fresh yeast   3 tablespoons castor sugar
30g (1oz) sugar
⅛ litre (¼ pint) warm milk   Glaze
1 beaten egg   2 tablespoons sugar
75g (2½oz) butter   3 tablespoons water

Sift the flour and salt into a bowl and make a well in the centre. Dissolve the yeast and 1 teaspoon of the sugar in a little of the warm milk. Cover and allow to stand till the yeast is bubbly. Now add the rest of the milk and the beaten egg to the yeast mixture and pour into the well in the flour. Halve the butter and shave one half over the flour. Combine the ingredients roughly with a wooden spoon and then turn out on a floured board and knead till the dough is smooth and elastic, taking up more flour in the process if necessary. Gather into a ball and place in a buttered bowl. Turn the dough ball so that all sides become evenly coated with butter. Prove till doubled in bulk. Punch down the dough and knead again lightly. Roll out to a rectangle measuring 25 × 40cm (10 × 16in). Melt the remaining butter and brush over the dough. Scatter the spice, currants and castor sugar evenly over the surface and roll up into a sausage, starting from the long side of the rectangle. Cut into 10–12 slices and place each slice on a greased baking sheet, leaving adequate room between the buns so that they will not touch each other after proving. Cover with a cloth and bake at 220°C/425°F for 20 minutes. While the Chelsea Buns are still warm brush with the glaze, which is made by boiling the sugar and water together till it forms a syrup, about 2 minutes. Dust with a little icing sugar shortly before serving.

PORTUGUESE HONEY BREAD

This is a highly spiced loaf which is usually made a week or two before being served. Try serving it with sangria or hot, sweet black coffee laced with a dash of whisky.

450g (1lb) butter	½ teaspoon baking powder
250g (9oz) sugar	¼ teaspoon black pepper
175ml (generous ¼ pint) molasses	1¾ tablespoons cinnamon
	2 teaspoons aniseed
80ml (⅛ pint) honey	¾ teaspoon ground cloves

½ cup walnut pieces
1 tablespoon finely chopped
candied lemon peel
3 tablespoons mixed chopped
glacé fruit

2 tablespoons of sweet sherry
or madeira
1 heaped tablespoon mashed
potato
750g (1lb 11oz) flour

Cream the butter and sugar with the molasses and honey till fluffy. Blend in everything bar the flour and beat till the mixture makes a smooth batter. Sift the flour over the cake batter, gradually incorporating it into the batter. Grease two deep loaf pans and fill each with half the mixture. Smooth the batter so that it is flat and bake for about 3 hours at 150°C/300°F. The cakes will be done when they are firm in the middle and shrinking from the sides of the tins.

BANANA TEA BREAD

This is a fruity, dark tea bread which gains in flavour as it ages. Try serving it with tea and rum on a cold afternoon, or in the evening with mulled wine.

300g (11oz) plain flour
½ teaspoon salt
1½ teaspoons baking powder
½ teaspoon bicarbonate of
soda
30g (1oz) butter

½ cup brown sugar
2 eggs
½ cup chopped walnuts
2 teaspoons grated orange peel
2 large mashed bananas

Sift the flour, salt, baking powder and soda together twice. Cream the butter and sugar, then add the beaten eggs and stir well. Stir in the nuts and orange rind. Add the flour mixture and bananas to the butter and sugar alternately, beating until smooth. Spoon into a greased baking form and bake at 180°C/350°F for about 1 hour.

BARMBRACK (Ireland)

The name of this Irish bread means literally 'aran breac', or spotted bread, because the loaves were speckled throughout with currants or aromatic seeds. It is meant to be eaten on All Saint's Day and is the fortune-teller of the coming year. For this reason, rings, coins or buttons are often baked in the dough to symbolize approaching marriage, wealth or blessings. Barmbrack is best eaten thinly sliced with butter spread liberally on each slice.

500g (1lb 2oz) currants
75g (2½oz) brown sugar
¼ litre (½ pint) cold, black tea

250g (9oz) flour
½ teaspoon baking powder
1 lightly-beaten egg

Soak the currants and brown sugar in the tea overnight. Sift the flour and baking powder together twice. Gradually add the flour to the soaked currants and tea, together with the beaten egg. Mix thoroughly and spoon into a greased tin. Bake at 190°C/375°F for about 1 hour.

CRUMPETS (England)

The English crumpet has long been the favourite of the afternoon tea table. Served with butter, piping hot and running with honey, it completes the picture of a family drawn up round the hearth in the late afternoon.

125g (4¼oz) flour
good pinch of salt
½ teaspoon sugar
15g (½oz) fresh yeast

a little lukewarm water
6 tablespoons warm milk
75g (2½oz) butter
1 egg

Sift the flour and salt into a bowl. Cream the sugar and yeast and dissolve in a little warm water. When dissolved, add the warm milk and pour into the centre of the flour. Mix the liquid with a little of the flour to form a paste, cover the bowl and allow to prove till the yeast is bubbly. Heat a quarter of the butter till melted and allow to cool to lukewarm. Crack the egg into the butter and beat till smooth. Now work the flour, yeast, egg and butter to a smooth dough by beating vigorously with a wooden spoon. Cover the bowl and let the batter prove till it is doubled in bulk. Melt the remaining butter and brush a large griddle or heavy frying pan and several crumpet rings or large scone cutters with some of it. Place the rings on the griddle and heat till the butter begins to sizzle. Drop 1 tablespoon of the proved dough into each ring and cook till the mixture bubbles and the crumpets are browned on their under surface. Turn the crumpets, ring and all and brown briefly on the other side. Continue in this manner, greasing the griddle and rings with each batch of crumpets. The crumpets can either be eaten immediately or stored and toasted as needed. Always serve hot with butter and honey or marmalade.

Chapter Six

'STALEMATE'

RECIPES FOR USING OLD OR STALE BREAD

Even the best loaf comes to an end sooner or later, and if later, one is often tempted to throw any lingering remnants away. A genuine bread lover never does this however as he has all sorts of delicious remedies when faced with a stalemate – he even uses the odd hunk of bread as an eraser, for which it is ideally suited. Here then are some thought-provoking recipes in which bread is used or used up.

BREAD SOUP RIGA (Latvia, USSR)

In Riga three races, languages and cuisines intermingle, and in the olden days a true man-of-Riga could greet his friends on the street in Russian, German or Latvian. This recipe is based on Russian Black bread and the addition of apples prevents it becoming heavy. It can also be made with white bread and milk.

250g (9oz) broken black or white bread
1 litre (1¾ pints) water
300g (11oz) peeled, cored apples

6 tablespoons raisins
sugar to taste
juice of ½ lemon

Simmer the black bread in water till soft. Lift the bread out of the water and force it through a sieve. Return the sieved bread to the water and slice the apples into it. Bring the soup to the boil and simmer till the apples are tender. Add the raisins and sugar and bring to the boil again. Remove from the heat and add the lemon juice.

BREAD SAUCE

1 *onion*	60g *(2oz) butter*
8 *cloves*	*salt*
125g *(4½oz) fresh white*	*pepper*
bread	*dash of cayenne pepper*
½ *litre (¾ pint) milk*	

Peel the onion and stick the cloves into it. Put the onion in a saucepan together with the other ingredients. Bring to the boil and then take away from the heat. Allow to steep for an hour. Remove the onion and bring the sauce to the boil again. Beat with a wooden spoon till smooth. Serve with poultry which has been stuffed with bread and sage.

BREAD AND BUTTER PUDDING

We've Puddin' here a treat,
We've Puddin' here galore;
Do not decline to stay and dine,
Our Puddin' you'll adore.

*   *   *

Eat away, chew away, munch and bolt and guzzle,
Never leave the table till you're full up to the muzzle.
The Magic Pudding – NORMAN LINDSAY

Fast disappearing from the modern culinary scene together with suet pudding and homemade gelatine, there was a time when bread and butter pudding was the mainstay of a nation. Little girls would be told by their nannies that it would make their hair curl if they ate it all up – the little boys were reminded in a quiet aside that it would put hair on their chest.

¼ litre (½ pint) milk	butter
4 eggs and 1 egg yolk	60g (2oz) dried, chopped
30g (1oz) sugar	fruit
¼ litre (½ pint) cream	¼ teaspoon vanilla essence
4 slices of white bread	nutmeg

Bring the milk almost to the boil. Beat the eggs and sugar together and pour the hot milk over them. Add the cream. Cut the crusts from the bread slices, butter them and place in the bottom of a greased baking dish. Sprinkle the chopped fruit over the bread and pour the milk into the dish. Stir in the vanilla, and while the custard is still swirling, sprinkle with nutmeg. Dot each slice of bread with a little butter. Place the dish in a large baking dish and fill the baking dish with enough water to come halfway up the sides of the pudding bowl. Bake at 180°C/350°F for an hour or until the pudding is set. If the pudding browns during baking, reduce the oven temperature.

HOUSKOVÉ KNEDLIKY
(Czechoslovakia)

These dumplings are cooked in long rolls and are then served sliced with butter. They are irresistible on a cold winter's day when served in the Czech manner with roast pork and creamed cabbage and caraway.

enough old white bread to measure a good ½ litre (¾ pint) in volume when diced (see below)	3 tablespoons potato flour, farina or cornflour
	½ teaspoon salt
	½ teaspoon baking powder
60g (2oz) butter	1 egg
350g (12oz) plain flour	¼ litre (½ pint) soda water

Cut the bread into cubes measuring 1cm (½in). Brown in the butter and reserve. Sift all the dry ingredients into a bowl and beat in the egg and soda water. Continue beating till the dough leaves the sides of the bowl. Cover and allow to stand for half an hour. Wet the hands and carefully incorporate the bread cubes into the dough. Bring a large saucepan of salted water to the boil and form the dough into two long rolls about 7½cm (3in) in diameter. Drop the rolls into the water which will then go off the boil. Bring the water to boiling point, cover the pot and allow the Houskové to simmer gently. Check the temperature of the water frequently during cooking as if it boils too fiercely the dumplings will break up. Cook for about 15 minutes and then rotate the rolls so that their other sides are uppermost. Simmer a further 15 minutes, then lift out of the water with a slotted spoon. Slice in finger-thick rounds and brush with melted butter. Serve with roast meat.

KIRSCHENMICHEL
Milk and Cherry Pudding (Germany)

For many centuries sugar was a costly and rare spice which was reserved for use on saints' days and holidays. In Franconia cooks substituted honey for sugar and learned to combine local berries such as the wood strawberry, elderberry and blueberry and sour cherry with milk and day-old bread to make a local dish known as a *Michel*.

> 2 *tablespoons honey*
> ¼ *litre (½ pint) hot milk*
> 4 *day-old white bread rolls*
> 100g (4oz) butter
>
> 4 *eggs*
> 1kg (2¼lb) *Morello cherries*
> *grated rind of one lemon*

Dissolve the honey in the milk and pour over the sliced rolls. Cream the butter and separate the eggs. Add the egg yolks to the butter and beat till smooth. Stir the cherries and lemon peel into the butter and yolk mixture. Beat the egg whites till they are very stiff; fold into the bread and fruit mixture and turn into a buttered baking dish. Dot with 25g (1oz) butter and bake at 200°C/400°F for 34–40 minutes.

FAIRY BREAD

'Come up here, O dusty feet!
Here is fairy bread to eat.
Here in my retiring room,
Children you may dine
On the golden smell of broom
And the shade of pine;
And when you have eaten well,
Fairy stories hear and tell.'

ROBERT LOUIS STEVENSON

Fairy bread is the timeless favourite at childrens' birthday parties, guaranteed to satisfy the child's eye and appetite without sending him home feeling bilious! Cut wafer thin, sprinkled liberally with hundreds-and-thousands and piled on a pretty plate, these colourful triangles of bread continue to tempt children of all ages.

1 *loaf of sandwich bread*
  (Pain de mie, see page 25*)*
butter

hundreds-and-thousands
  (nonpareils)

Cut the bread thinly and butter. Sprinkle with hundreds-and-thousands and cut diagonally into two pieces. Pile on a plate in a decorative pattern.

CROUSTADE

The croustade is a type of timbale or pie, whereby the case, instead of being made of pastry is made of bread. The croustade can be of any shape or size and is filled with creamed vegetables, ragoût or sea foods. Small bread rolls make ideal hors d'oeuvres croustades or can be served individually as entrées.

> 1 *day-old or stale sandwich*   *butter or fat for frying*
> *loaf (Pain de mie) or*
> *several stale bread rolls*

If making a large croustade, score the outside of the loaf with a decorative pattern and, with the point of a sharp knife, mark a wide slice from the top of the loaf. (This will form the lid after the loaf has been fried.) If making smaller croustades from bread rolls, score the roll around the middle so that it can easily be hollowed out after cooking. Deep fry the loaves in fat, oil or butter till golden. Drain on paper towels and cut off the lid of the croustade where marked, prior to frying. Hollow out the loaf from the inside, being careful not to break the walls of the croustade. Fill the croustade with the required filling and warm in the oven till it is to be served.

Croustade d'Orsay

The 'd'Orsay' was once a well known Parisian câfé where numerous memorable concoctions found their origin, amongst them the Vol-au-Vent d'Orsay, the filling of which is just at home in a croustade as in a vol-au-vent.

> 1 *large croustade, or 6 small*   2 *cloves*
> *croustades*   1½ *tablespoons flour*
> 10 *artichoke hearts*   ¼ *litre (½ pint) veal and*
> 250g *(9oz) champignons*   *carrot stock*
> *(use only the true*   *sweet paprika*
> *champignon or 'button*   ½ *bay leaf*
> *mushroom')*   500g *(1lb 2oz) cooked*
> *butter*   *chicken breast*
> 75g *(2½oz) bacon*   *sour cream*
> 1 *small chopped onion*   *pepper and salt*

Prepare the croustade as given above. Steam the artichoke hearts and sliced champignons till tender and reserve. Place 30g (1oz) butter in a heavy saucepan and melt. Add the finely chopped bacon and onion, the cloves and bay leaf, cover with a round of greaseproof paper and sweat gently till the onion is transparent. Stir in 1½ tablespoons flour and cook the roux gently till it gives off a nutty perfume. Add the stock, paprika and bay leaf and bring to the boil, stirring all the time. Lower the heat and add the diced chicken, champignons and artichoke hearts. Cover the saucepan and cook very gently for 5 minutes. Stir in enough sour cream to flavour and bind the sauce. Correct seasoning. Fill the croustade and serve after it is heated through.

Quail Croustade

The quail is a small bird, much prized by connoisseurs for its delicate flavour. Although the birds are often trapped and caged on their migratory flights between Europe and Africa in order to be fattened, it is a well known fact that any naturally wild animal will lose its gamey taste once it is brought into captivity – this has been the case in Japan where deer are bred on farms. If you are lucky enough to live in the country or to have a father-in-law who, like mine, is a forester you may be able to hunt your own quail, in which case, remember that the quail must hang for longer than 3 days but not so long as to be 'high' as in the case of larger game.

The following recipe will fill one croustade or several smaller ones.

2–3 *quails*	*a few chopped truffles*
salt and pepper	100g *(4oz) ground cooked*
butter for frying	*veal*
1 *finely chopped onion*	2 *chicken livers*
100g *(4oz) thinly sliced ham*	¼ *litre (½ pint) veal stock*
	a good dash of brandy

Prepare the croustade and set aside. Bone the quails, season the meat with pepper and salt and fry gently in butter on all sides for 5 minutes. Lift out the meat and add the chopped onion, ham, truffles, veal and chicken livers to the pan. Cook in the butter being careful not to brown the onion, for 5 minutes. Return the quail to the pan and add the veal stock. Correct the seasoning and pour in a good dash of brandy. Cover the saucepan and cook the sauce very gently till the quail meat is tender. Thicken the sauce with a little *beurre manié*, made by kneading 30g (1oz) butter with one tablespoon of flour. Fill the croustade with the quail ragoût and warm in the oven till heated through.

TOASTS

When preparing toast in the English manner, be sure that the toast is brought hot and steaming to the table. Never wrap it in a cloth to keep it warm, as this makes it leathery. Day-old bread is said to make the best toast, but this is purely a matter of taste. On the Continent toast is only made from white bread, but it is delicious and unusual made from any of the darker breads.

French Toast
Heat butter in a frying pan and brown the toast in it on both sides. If meat has been prepared by frying, bread can be fried in the fat used for the meat.

Melba Toast
Slice white bread thinly and cut away the crusts. Place the slices on a baking sheet and bake in a slow oven till golden. Store in air-tight jars. Melba toast is excellent served with pâté or soups.

Cinnamon Toast
Toast white bread, butter generously while still hot and sprinkle with a mixture of cinnamon and white sugar.

CROÛTONS

The classical French accompaniment to soup of all kinds, the croûtons are fried in butter and served plain, or can be sprinkled with parmesan cheese before they are cooked for more flavour. Three croûtons are placed in the middle of each bowl of soup, the rest being served separately on a plate.

several slices of white bread
fat or butter for frying

optional grated parmesan cheese

Cut the crusts away from the bread slices and cut each slice into small dice. Heat the fat or butter till it sizzles and fry the bread dice till they are golden on all sides. Drain on paper towels before serving, and sprinkle with parmesan cheese if desired.

BREADCRUMBS

Dry slices of white bread in the oven till just golden. Crush with a rolling pin and store in air-tight jars.

WHAT TO DO WITH LEFT-OVER YEAST – GINGER BEER

If you find at the end of a bread-making session that you have a small remnant of fresh yeast, why not make some ginger beer with it? It is inexpensive and makes a cooling summer drink. Served with a good dollop of vanilla ice cream it is unforgettable! If you are worried that the bottles will explode in your face (I worry), try bottling the beer in large plastic bottles which have an airtight seal, or open the bottles cautiously and if they seem to be letting-off great quantities of carbon dioxide gas, stand them in the sink and open by degrees to release the gas slowly – this will ensure that a volcano of beer will not spurt as high as the ceiling. Of course the best advice of all is to make the ginger beer in quantities which can be quickly used up.

$7\frac{1}{2}g$ ($\frac{1}{4}oz$) dry yeast   ginger
1 cup warm water   5 litres (9 pints) water
sugar $\frac{1}{8}$ litre ($\frac{1}{4}$ pint) lemon juice

Dissolve the yeast in 1 cup warm water and add 2 teaspoons sugar. Stir and cover with a piece of muslin. For one week feed the plant daily with 1 teaspoon of ginger and 2 tea-spoons sugar. On the eighth day, dissolve 800g (1lb 12oz) sugar in 1 litre ($1\frac{3}{4}$ pints) of boiling water. Pour into a large, clean plastic bucket and add the lemon juice; stir to dissolve. Pour off the liquid from the top of the ginger plant, leaving the dregs to start a fresh brew, and add to the hot water in the bucket. Stir thoroughly. Add 4 litres (7 pints) of cold water and stir again. Bottle the ginger beer and seal. After four or five days it will be ready to drink.

Table of Comparative Measures

	Metric	British	American
FLUID	1 litre	1¾ pints	4¼ cups or 1 quart 2 ounces
	½ litre or 500 millilitres	¾ pint (generous)	2 cups* (generous) or 1 pint
	⅛ litre or 125 millilitres	1 gill ¼ pint (scant) 5 fluid ounces	½ cup or ¼ pint
	1/10 litre or 100 millilitres	3–4 ounces	½ cup (scant) or ¼ pint (scant)
WEIGHTS	28 grams	1 ounce	1 ounce
	100 grams	3½ ounces	3½ ounces
	225 grams	8 ounces	8 ounces
	500 grams	1 pound 1½ ounces	1 pound 1½ ounces
ALMONDS	150 grams	5½ ounces	1 cup
BAKING POWDER	5 grams	1 teaspoon	1 teaspoon
BREADCRUMBS	100 grams	3½ ounces	1 cup (generous)
BUTTER	30 grams	1 ounce	2 tablespoons
	125 grams	4 ounces (generous)	½ cup or 1 stick
	500 grams	1 pound (generous)	2 cups

* The American and Canadian Standard cup has a capacity of 8 fluid ounces.

Table of Comparative Measures

	Metric	British	American
CORNFLOUR OR ARROWROOT	10 grams	⅓ ounce	1 tablespoon
FLOUR	500 grams	1 pound (generous)	3½ cups
DRIED FRUITS	500 grams	1 pound (generous)	2 cups
RAISINS SULTANAS CURRANTS	500 grams	1 pound	3 cups
SALT	15 grams	½ ounce	1 tablespoon
SPICES	15 grams	½ ounce	2 tablespoons
SUGAR	5 grams 250 grams	⅙ ounce 8 ounces	1 teaspoon 1 cup (generous)
SUGAR POWDERED	150 grams	5 ounces	1 cup (generous)
SUGAR BROWN	150 grams	5 ounces	1 cup (generous)
YEAST DRIED	7½ grams	¼ ounce	1 cake or envelope* yeast
YEAST FRESH	28 grams	1 ounce	1 ounce
TEMPERATURES	60 deg. C 100 deg. C 200 deg. C	140 deg. F 212 deg. F 400 deg. F	140 deg. F 212 deg. F 400 deg. F

* Dried yeast has half the weight of fresh yeast.

BIBLIOGRAPHY

The Bible
'The World we have lost', Peter Lazlett.
'Backen mit Lust und Liebe', Roland Göök.
'Gourmet', Cookbooks and Magazines
'Beard on Bread', James Beard
'Fachkunde für Bäcker', Hilfbücher der Österreichische
    Gewerbe
'Use Your Loaf', U. and D. Norman.
Larousse, Gastronomique
'The Cooking of The British Isles', Time Life Books
'Das Elektrische Kochen', Elizabeth Meyer-Haagen
'Die Zeit', German Weekly Newspaper
'Household Management', Mrs Beeton
'Das Paradiesische Apfel', Heimeran Verlag
Biblical Dictionary, ed. Edinburgh, 1875
'Elle', French weekly magazine
'History of England', Trevelyan

INDEX

Jean Conil

THE MAGNUM COOKBOOK

The Magnum Cookbook is a must for all serious cooks. It contains a wide variety of recipes ranging from the basic to exotic, as well as exciting recipes for special occasions. Roast beef and Yorkshire pudding and a host of other traditional English recipes are included.

Master Chef Jean Conil's experience as a chef and nutritionist has enabled him to write a comprehensive book covering all aspects of cookery. He outlines the basic 'do's' and 'don'ts' of which every cook should be aware; a knowledge which he hopes will give confidence and inspiration to develop new ideas in the kitchen.

Carolyn McCrum

THE SOUP BOOK

Soup is a versatile food suitable for all occasions. A delicate consommé will make a fine start to a rich meal; an iced soup is wonderfully refreshing on a summer's day; and a meat soup can satisfy the heartiest appetite as a complete meal on a winter's night.

In **The Soup Book** Carolyn McCrum explains the basic methods and essential equipment for stock and soup-making. There are many recipes ranging from simple soups that can be prepared in minutes to elaborate soups like the famed Bouillabaise, Pot-au-Feu and Gazpacho. Favourite soups are included as well as new ideas, such as Iced Coconut and Aubergine Soup.

Jan Hopcraft

COOKING TODAY, EATING TOMORROW

Do you like to cook for your friends but always find yourself too rushed to enjoy it? This bestselling cookery book is designed for busy people. The recipes are clearly presented in the form of menus for dinner, lunch and fork supper parties. No menu contains more than one dish which has to be made from start to finish on the actual day. Each recipe has been specially designed to cut right down on time spent in the kitchen at the last minute, so that you can enjoy more time with your guests.

ENTERTAINING ON A BUDGET

A practical guide to tempting yet inexpensive meals for entertaining. Jan Hopcraft demonstrates that lashings of wine and cream are not essential for a first-class meal. She uses cider and a wide range of herbs and spices to transform simple ingredients into delicious and exciting dishes. These imaginative recipes include totally new ideas as well as traditional dishes and advice on cutting costs. Many dishes can be prepared in advance, making this an essential cookery book for those who have to economise on time as well as cost.

Other Wine and Cookery Books available from Magnum Books

These and other Magnum Books are available at your bookshop or newsagent. In case of difficulties orders may be sent to:

Magnum Books
Cash Sales Department
PO Box 11
Falmouth
Cornwall TR10 109EN

Please send cheque or postal order, no currency, for purchase price quoted and allow the following for postage and packing:

U.K.   25p for the first book plus 10p per copy for each additional book ordered to a maximum of £1.05.

B.F.P.O. & Eire   25p for the first book plus 10p per copy for the next 8 books, thereafter 5p per book.

Overseas customers   40p for the first book and 12p per copy for each additional book.

While every effort is made to keep prices low, it is sometimes necessary to increase price at short notice. Magnum Books reserve the right to show new retail prices on covers which may differ from those previously advertised in the text or elsewhere.